ARMISTEAD
MAUPIN

Other works by Patrick Gale
(published by Flamingo unless otherwise stated)

The Aerodynamics of Pork
Ease
Kansas in August
Facing the Tank
Little Bits of Baby
Caesar's Wife from the collection Secret Lives
(Serpents Tail)
The Cat Sanctuary
The Facts of Life
Dangerous Pleasures (short stories) ·
Tree Surgery for Beginners
(Published in US by Faber & Faber)

All photographs courtesy of the Armistead Maupin Collection, used with permission.

Painting on page 48 reproduced with kind permission from David Hockney.
Drawing on page 102 reproduced with kind permission from Don Bachardy.

Outlines

ARMISTEAD MAUPIN

PATRICK GALE

Absolute Press

First published in 1999 by Absolute Press
Scarborough House, 29 James Street West,
Bath, Somerset, England BA1 2BT
Tel: 01225 316013 Fax: 01225 445836
Email: outlines@absolute press.demon.co.uk

Distributed in the United States of America and Canada by
Stewart, Tabori and Chang
115 West 18th Street, New York, NY 10011

© Patrick Gale 1999
Armistead Maupin's Design for Living first appeared
in The Advocate and is reproduced by kind permission of the author.

The rights of Patrick Gale to be identified as author of this
work have been asserted by him in accordance with the
Copyright Designs and Patents Act 1988

Series editor Nick Drake

Cover and text design by Ian Middleton

Cover printed by Devenish and Co. Bath
Printed by The Cromwell Press, Trowbridge

ISBN 1 899791 37 X

Contents

JANE, TEDDY AND TONY, AS POSED BY ARMISTEAD SR, ON THE BATTLEFIELD IN
ANTIETAM, VIRGINIA, WHERE THEIR GREAT, GREAT GRANDFATHER FELL IN 1862.
ONE OF THE MANY PHALLIC SYMBOLS THEY WERE CALLED UPON TO WORSHIP

Introduction

This won't be a traditional biography. If you're after what Nancy Reagan, referring in a rare moment of wit to Ms Kelly's infamous hatchet job, called Kitty Litter, you'll just have to wait. I think it was the biographer Brenda Maddox who said that the trouble with homosexual biography is that it tends to fall into overlapping narratives rather than an easily assimilated line. Where even a philandering straight subject will tend to have a succession of mistresses or a succession of wives, gay lives, especially gay lives before the mid-1970s, tend to be lived several at a time. Official lovers, rough lovers, family, non family, those who know, those who don't; the mere fact of the subject's alternative sexuality causes narrative fractures. Of course, one of the most liberating aspects of a gay life, the aspect which Armistead Maupin has repeatedly made available to straight readers, is the way in which, as he says of his character, Mouse, 'You can be a cute little clone in the San Francisco Gay Chorus and yet spin into Rock Hudson's orbit.'

So. No straight lines here but a succession of overlapping tales. It's a form, too, which reflects the book's friendly, conversational source. I stopped off in San Francisco on my way home from a gruelling Australian book tour and we spent hours of the next ten days lolling on sofas gossiping about everything from why Armistead understood *precisely* why Monica would have enjoyed sex with the President, to which gay novelists we were wary of and why. We discussed why so many gay affairs subside into friendship, whether cranberry Newtons are superior to fig ones and just which stars were ripe to follow the Heche-Degeneresses out of the well-appointed Hollywood closet. Occasionally we would fall silent to watch Todd, the ludicrously sexy gay gardener, getting muddy among the tree ferns and occasionally we would remember that we were there to discuss Armistead's life, work and loves. There was even a Los Angeles interlude, to see how *Armistead Maupin's More*

Tales of the City fared at the Emmy Awards and to celebrate David Hockney's unveiling of his vast Grand Canyon landscape. It was enormous fun, hideously revealing for both of us – even though Armistead is a pass-master at ducking issues I found myself as merciless as a dentist in pursuing them - and apparently the process helped him to wrestle with the more painful autobiographical elements in *The Night Listener*, his novel-in-progress.

Unless I say otherwise, therefore, everything in quotation marks is Armistead speaking, lifted from the hours and hours of tapes I ended up having to transcribe.

I was asked to write a book that was as much about our friendship as it was about the man himself, but I suspect there is enough evidence of our friendship in the stories I have winkled out and the tone in which I tell them. Besides, in the immortal words of Roseanne, 'This is *so* not about you, Jackie!' Neither have I written in any critical detail about the novels on which Armistead's gay icon status rests. The chances are that if you're reading this book it's because you already know the work and would like a closer encounter with the man. If not, then put this down immediately, go to the M shelf of the fiction section and buy the things. They will do the job of explaining their quirky appeal far better than I could.

We met back in 1988 when we were both deeply in love, each with men who would change our lives, to whom we would dedicate several novels and with whom we would move to remote rustic corners. We had loved each other's books and had said so in print – always a good start – and he and his lover, Terry Anderson, invited me and the other Patrick (Pender) to an extraordinary party in Hockney's Kensington studio where we took turns in trying on a collection of famous spectacles and I only just dissuaded a drunken girlfriend from making off with a stash of unsigned phone-pad doodles. Since then it has been, perforce, a friendship of late-night phone calls – he's a hopeless correspondent – and precious holiday visits which invariably end with me wanting to move to San Francisco and him encouraging me and me being far too cowardly to go through with it.

We have a running joke that there is a Maupin curse that dooms my relationship
with any lover I take to visit him. Twice I have subjected him to tense
encounters because the lover I booked a trip with had transmuted into a friend
by the time we arrived. This time I was travelling alone, albeit with the
bittersweet pleasure of sustaining a fresh romance by e-mail, and I made the most
of it, doing no sightseeing whatsoever and only venturing out to eat or to walk
Sophie, his newly acquired and utterly harebrained Australian Shepherd mix.

Arriving chez Maupin from rural Cornwall is like landing on the moon and
in quite the wrong clothes. It always takes some time to adjust. It's not just
the jet lag. For the first day I invariably feel like some wide-eyed provincial
drawn, dazzled, into Mrs Madrigal's orbit. However hard I try not to let my
parental conditioning show, I come across about as hip as Cleveland in
February. There's the pot. My drug of choice is chocolate but Armistead's
place is a fat-free zone so he offers liberal quantities of pot as soon as work is
done. And yes, I inhale and yes, it makes me impossibly giggly. Then there's
the hot tub in the garden. Where I come from we bathe frequently – farms
are dirty places – but we do it indoors and we do it unaccompanied. Then
there are all those little things to trap the uncool unwary. In 1981 two gay
San Franciscans were caught up in a hijacked aeroplane drama in Beirut and
Armistead had to lead the party of local celebrities who welcomed the
unlikely heroes back to the Castro with a brass band. His mind wasn't on the
job because he was late for a circle jerk up the hill. He had to run all the way
there and barely tore his clothes off in time. And that was where he met José,
who has been his housekeeper ever since. On my planet housekeepers are
usually female, come with reputable references, and aren't half so much fun.
They certainly don't discuss their latest tattoo or the revolutionary effect of
Viagra on the Glory Holes with a newly arrived house guest ...

Before you read the result of ten day's self-indulgence, let's get one thing
clear. The name. It is not pronounced with a French accent, so as to rhyme
with Gaugin. Think Somerset Maugham. Better yet, imitate Vivien Leigh
describing what Butterfly MacQueen might to do the kitchen floor and you'll
be nearer the mark.

PORTRAIT BY ROBERT SKEMP OF ARMISTEAD SR IN HUNTING GARB

Big Armistead and Diana

Armistead Jones Maupin Jr sprang upon an unsuspecting world at Doctors Hospital in Washington DC. The year being 1944, his father was a skipper on a minesweeper at the time, so gathered the news by semaphore and didn't actually see his son for almost two years. Armistead has always loved the idea of his arrival being announced, *South Pacific* style, by a hunky young sailor waving white flags and has seized on the image as the perfect metaphor for the difficulty this particular father and son would always have in communicating directly. 'It's like "I'm waving! Do you read me? Basic emotion! Basic emotion!"'

Armistead was brought home to 511 Cameron Street in Alexandria, Virginia, the house where the Scottish Rite, the official Masonic ritual of America, was established. His mother lived there with her own widowed mother and assorted siblings until his father returned from the war.

The three adults would be Armistead's greatest influences. Armistead Sr – or Big Armistead as he was called to differentiate him from his son – was a fiery lawyer of aristocratic Southern stock, intensely proud of his antecedents. His wife, Diana Jane Barton, was of English stock, a kind-hearted beauty who eventually established a chapter of the SPCA (Society for the Prevention of Cruelty to Animals). Her British-born mother, Marguerite Smith Barton, a former women's suffragist who had married a Victorian patriarch thirty years her senior, was a charmingly eccentric widow infatuated with theosophy and palm-reading. Both women found in amateur theatricals the time-honoured relief for those hemmed in by the demands of respectability.

Armistead swiftly became known as Teddy. Officially this was just another way to distinguish him from his old man, but the choice bothered his father,

Armistead recalls, because his mother had once had a boyfriend named Ted. For his part, Armistead called his parents Mummie and Daddy, in the English fashion, then – when other boys teased him for this – Mither and Pap.

His paternal grandmother, Mary Armistead Maupin, who later came to live with the family, was known as Mimi. The granddaughter of a confederate general, Mimi was Armistead's living link with his Southern roots. 'She was this sweet twinkly-eyed little thing who laughed a lot and told great stories about Sherman's army, and as a girl she had actually ridden on Jefferson Davis's casket when it passed through town.'

When Armistead Sr left the Navy, the family settled where the Maupin roots lay, in Raleigh, North Carolina. 312 Forest Road was a white frame duplex in an old neighbourhood. His first best friend was the girl next door, Kathy Austin, who took enormous pleasure in dressing him in her doll's clothes, Armistead being a fully co-operative stooge. Later he asked his parents for a doll's house, not for the feminine pleasure of dolls but as a stage setting for the little plays he would put on. He also fashioned theatres from cardboard boxes from the Piggly Wiggly, making puppets and learning to sew them costumes, with reassuring crudity.

His theatrical bent was encouraged when Diana went for an audition at the Raleigh Little Theatre for the part of Medea. The company couldn't take her this time but they said they could 'use the kid' for the non-speaking part of one of Jason's murdered sons. So he made his theatrical debut aged six, despite giggling fits when his friend Nat Robb had to lie on top of him. 'That backstage to me was a place of tremendous mystery and wonder. It was built on a hillside and you descended through dressing rooms until you got to the green room which opened out onto a garden. So the whole thing was sort of labyrinthine and spooky. I had dreams about it for years. I still do. I learned at a very early age that I could take refuge in that kind of fantasy.'

The family rented at first but once Armistead Sr had joined the law firm in which he would rise to be head partner, they began to build the house where Armistead Sr still lives, a rambling ranch house in a woody dell with a creek below it. Armistead remembers his father's repeated attempts to dam the creek in the hope of creating a lake. Whenever a big storm broke, the waters would swell and begin to burst holes in the dam, leaving Armistead Sr raging about the place, tearing out pieces of the basement storeroom in his futile attempts to shore up his handiwork. 'We all thought it was funny and kind of sweet in a Zorba-like way. And I helped him with the dam. That was one of the things, one of the few things we had, that really bonded us. I loved to hang out with him in the garden where he was constantly building rock walls and working on that dam. He had a very strong aesthetic sense when it came to the garden.'

Diana supplied her firstborn with a brother and sister, four and five years younger, called Tony and Jane. They were duly corralled into his impromptu circus acts, theatre shows and woodland fantasies, forming a part of what he remembers as an idyllic childhood. The only black spots were the three or four times he was sent off to summer camp. 'I found it completely agonizing because I was forced into an all-boy fascist society in which I excelled at nothing. And I missed my family terribly.'

Then there was the recurring thundercloud of his father's anger. 'His rages could be sudden and frightening and completely inexplicable until I got older and learned what he'd been through himself.' Diana would smooth things over after these explosions, becoming what Armistead describes as his father's 'official apologist'. 'She spent a great deal of time saying, 'Your father really loves you. I know it doesn't always seem so but he really does. You have to understand that about him.' Which Armistead learned to do. 'There was a song from *The King and I*, the one where the long-suffering head wife sings about the King and says, "He may not always do what you would have him do, but now and then he'll do something wonderful." I applied that to my father. That was the way I explained him to myself.'

God was ever present but unobtrusive; Armistead was raised what he calls a *social* Episcopalian. 'We went once a week and we'd go for Christmas Eve but the only religious instruction my mother ever gave me was when periodically she would turn to me in church and say, 'Look *reverent!*' because she was aware that other people were watching. Even the pew we sat in was a matter of social status. It had belonged to our family for years. It was the Maupin pew. And years later, when our churchgoing began to fall off because no one in the family had a drop of spiritual blood, other people started using the pew, and I can remember my father rounding us all up in the house in a fit of desperation and saying, 'If we don't get down there in the next fifteen goddammed minutes, that housepainter and his wife are going to take the goddammed pew!'

Episcopalians in the early Sixties, whatever their political colour, would scorn religious fundamentalists as white trash types who didn't see the fun of gambling and drink. Armistead Sr had inherited the family's tradition of cavalierly Rabelaisian attitudes and, for all his social pride, had a horror of priggishness. He was fond of talking to his boys about *poontang* – the Southern corruption of *putain* once used to denote a black whore but later applied to pussy in general. He also liked to rouse them of a morning with a cry of 'Reveille! Reveille! All hands heave to and trice up. Drop your cocks and grab your socks!' a speech he would occasionally enhance by delivering it with a tee shirt hanging off his morning glory.

A girlfriend of Armistead's nicknamed his parents John Wayne and Auntie Mame. Armistead Sr may not have joined in the fun at the Raleigh Little Theatre, but it's surely no accident that in every anecdote, the man has an audience. 'He demands to be the centre of attention,' Armistead admits, 'And he's probably not the only member of the family who turned out that way ...' Armistead Sr's views were extreme to the point of theatricality and he took pride in taking public stands. Armistead liked to see his father as a vivid Southern lawyer with a sense of justice, a man in the Atticus Finch mould, as he seemed when he made the front page of the newspaper by defending the right of neighbourhood dogs to roam unleashed. 'He was my hero, and I mimicked his conservative politics until I began to be bothered by his racism. He would rant about "niggers" and Jews and fairies and anyone else who was different. He still does – just doesn't include fairies, of course, when I'm around. Sometimes I think he does it just to get a reaction. I never saw him be anything but gracious to strangers.'

Diana was not really an Auntie Mame. She lacked the freedom of spirit. For all that she cultivated a fey, theatrical side, she grew more and more like her husband politically, 'Less because she believed in it, I think, than because she loved him. They did everything together. When I was in college they even started riding to hounds together. It was a drag hunt – one where they chased just the scent of a fox – but every now and then they'd flush out a real one and my mother would be bereft for weeks. She hated causing pain to anything or anyone.' Armistead adored her and refers to her as 'the Caretaker'. Throughout his childhood she had people in her life the family nicknamed her Refugees. These were usually European women who had married Southerners in the fond hope of a gracious, antebellum lifestyle only to find themselves shackled to some redneck in a rustic shack. Diana gave them emotional support and friendship in return for a taste, however ersatz, of European sophistication. Something of an outsider in the South, Diana retained an accent that was neither English nor Southern but vaguely Greer Garson. 'She remained, to all intents and purposes, a little English girl who'd grown up in the mountains of North Carolina with very odd English parents.'

Until he was twelve, Armistead attended Ravenscroft, the Episcopal parochial school in downtown Raleigh. It consisted of a small chapel, a school building and a Quonset hut where most of the classes were held. He recalls a female art teacher who tied boys to a lavatory as a punishment but has no other grim memories of it. 'It was just school. I went to school with the same thirty people for the first six grades. I knew them very well. I knew that the girls in that class were going to make their debut when they arrived at the age of eighteen. My parents loved the fact that I was there because I was being educated with members of my own class.' One teacher used to hand out a picture postcard to each pupil and make them write three paragraphs describing what they saw. She constantly singled Armistead out as the best at this exercise, which was his first awareness that he was clever with words. Left-handed and hopelessly unathletic, he routinely found himself picked after the girls when teams were being formed for sports. (A bittersweet torture, aged thirteen, was when he played the kidnapped son in a Raleigh Little Theatre production of Joseph Hayes' *The Desperate Hours*. Being roughed up and abducted by hunky, grown-up men was a delight. Having to make an entrance tossing a football while believably delivering the line: 'We've got a big game today and we're going to murder 'em,' was quite another matter ...) Happily his father was no sportsman either and hated guns (for reasons that would become clear later) so Armistead's family never made him feel inadequate in this regard or expected him to go on hunting trips.

Ravenscroft had its camp side. In the final year, the sixth grade, pupils were encouraged to dance with each other during the morning break. Desks would be cleared away and boys and girls would change into Bermuda shorts – the new fashion rage – and for half an hour do the Bop to records. His ally at these times was the tomboy of his year, although she grew impatient with his bopping on one occasion and humiliated him by picking him bodily off the ground and dropping him on the dance floor. (Six years later, striving for heterosexuality, he disastrously groped her in his Volkswagen in the parking lot of the Carolina Country Club, an event that was rehashed to great hilarity in the late Eighties when the two were reunited as gay activists. 'It was the worst night of *her* life, too.')

At thirteen, Armistead faced the grim prospect of entering the public school system. Josephus Daniels Junior High School was still white – segregation remained in force – and predominantly middle class, but the social mix was far wider and he was no longer cozily surrounded by Episcopalians. The pressure on boys and girls to date from the moment they entered the seventh grade was enormous. Armistead had learned to wank that summer at Camp Hemlock and had found he was far more aroused by the sight of his stud-muffin counsellor – 'His name, for the record, was Tollie Barbour' – than by the girls at the neighbouring camp.

But he consoled himself with the thought that he just hadn't met the right girl yet. 'I knew my father hadn't married my mother until he was twenty-six, so I told myself I had some time to work this thing out. I had an idealized girlfriend who was going to look a little bit like Grace Kelly and a little bit like Kim Novak. Of course no-one in the world looked a little bit like either of them so it was a pretty safe bet. And I was constantly inventing aristocratic names for our children-to-be. I became very good at the art of camouflage. I learned to pay attention to girls in a rude way in the presence of boys.'

Meanwhile he began to have sex dreams about men, especially older ones such as the gas station attendants he would eyeball around Raleigh, or the barber whose thigh would occasionally brush against Armistead's hand as he leaned in to clip his hair. He managed to justify these to himself, 'Because it was just about sex; it was the sort of diddling that all boys did and it was okay.' The dreams only caused him panic when kissing entered their scenarios. 'I knew something was seriously wrong because there was a romantic element attached to it. It wasn't just messing around; it was *romance* of the kind that you had with girls, and that scared the hell out of me. I'd read somewhere that homosexuality was a mental illness, so I tried to work up the nerve to tell my parents before it was too late to fix me. But the thought of doing that was too frightening.'

I'm the luckiest gay man I know in that fate allowed me a gay adolescence synchronized with my biological one. It's the rarity of this that lies behind Armistead's activism on behalf of gay youth movements; he believes one of the continuing tragedies of gay culture is that most of us are still working through our emotional adolescence at the age of thirty.

Giggling at the memory, we exchange horror stories of growing up gay in strait-laced provincial towns. I recall hanging around in W H Smiths plucking up courage to snatch a copy of *Playgirl* and glancing through it with hot cheeks while standing safely under *Motorsport and Railway Modeller*. Armistead remembers walking into a news-stand in a seedy Raleigh hotel in 1965 – he was 21 – and spotting a magazine called *Demigod*. 'And on the cover was a man – I'm sure he would look quite ordinary today – sitting up in bed, bare chested, with a yellow satin sheet pulled up to his waist. And the very fact of the intentional homoeroticism of that imagery just made me go nuts. I could barely glance at it and I certainly wouldn't have looked inside it. I just looked at the cover and thought "Oh. My. God." It was a very hot, steamy day and I remember going back to my car and turning on the radio and 'Walk on the Wild Side' was playing. Oh but it seems so quaint now!'

Hard to remember, now that it's so prevalent, but the fetishizing of the male body which our cultures do in general now is still a recent phenomenon.

Playgirl aside, my main erotic outlets as a child were reproductions of pictures by Botticelli and Leonardo in a couple of treasured Phaidon hardbacks. Armistead had to make do with Ronald Reagan and the desexed, knitting pattern idols of the late Fifties, Rock Hudson being a notable exception. I admit to having spent hours as a young boy leafing through old *Good Housekeeping* copies in search of the occasional man in a towel advertising a shower cubicle. 'Yeah,' Armistead admits, 'I used to think to myself as an early teenager: "I must be really sick. I'm looking at men's chests. Men's chests aren't supposed to be sexy. Only women's chests are supposed to be sexy."' A culture that was defined by straight, white males didn't even *part* with the information.'

Ironically, it was Armistead's parents who encouraged his fantasy life by giving him a copy of a novel by Allen Drury called *Advise and Consent* which they felt to be a highly moral good read. This is a conservative political thriller in which the young senator hero is blackmailed about a 'homosexual episode' in his past. The episode, described with preposterous coyness to modern eyes, involves his discreetly picking up another man on a beach in Honolulu during World War II. 'He's looking across at this man and realizing that "there was a similar hunger in his eyes" or some such phraseology and moments later they get up and walk to the hotel. That was the extent of the homoeroticism in the novel and the rest of it was left up to your imagination. It was the most powerfully affirming thing I had ever read. It was wonderful just to have the acknowledgement that such a moment could occur.' A few years later Armistead would see the film version of *Advise and Consent* and be completely horrified by its depiction of a gay night-club. 'It seemed so sleazy and awful to me, and it struck terror in my heart because I thought that's where I was headed. And after I came out and became an activist I thought of that scene as a homophobic distortion until I looked at it again for *The Celluloid Closet* and realized it was really rather tame. It was my fear I'd remembered, not the scene itself.'

But we agree that there was always a huge divide, when we were growing up, between the profoundly depressing, shabby images of homosexuality in films and the electric eroticism and romantic charge we could glean from our private reading. Partly because novels were always less censored than films but also, perhaps, because even then we were embryo novelists, reading between the lines of a text and overlaying the imaginative imagery that best matched our emerging desires.

I meanwhile was blessed with the kind of English father who had a horror of any kind of nakedly emotional discussion and who therefore left me to my own erotic devices. Poor Armistead had not only the pressures of the high school dating war but a father who teased him about wanking in the bathroom and, while not quite leading him to the nearest whorehouse calling out, 'Break him in, Lola,' encouraged him to sow wild oats and did it with a certain relish. 'I don't care who you screw, son, just don't bring her home,' he would say jovially.

Needless to say, respectable Raleigh offered no suitable role models for the gay teen. Diana had a dressmaker who looked and sounded like Liberace, 'a terrifying creature' openly mocked by Armistead Sr as 'a fairy nice fellow'. As were the numerous gay men involved in Diana's amateur theatricals at the Raleigh Little Theatre. There was a scandal in Armistead's scout troop when an adult leader was fired for 'interfering' with one of the boys. (Armistead himself had dreamed of interfering with this boy.) Beyond this, weekly scout meetings were a kind of purgatory. 'It was just one more controlled fascist state. Every week there was something called a belt line in which one boy, who was deemed to be insubordinate, would be forced to run down between two lines of boys who had taken their belts off and would whip his butt until he got to the end. I don't know *what* was on the mind of the scoutmaster who cooked *that* one up ...'

Another shadow over his high school years was the discovery that his paternal grandfather, dead before his parents met, had committed suicide. Armistead only found out at fifteen because a schoolfriend was drawn into a fight defending Armistead's Sr's honour against someone who had referred to him as 'the suicide's son'. The story was that Armistead Sr was hauled out of a university class by an ancient family retainer who bluntly told him his daddy 'done killed hisself', thereby converting a callow youth into the man of the house. Diana only sketched in the facts, leaving her son all the more puzzled. 'It became this enormous pink elephant that was in the room with us all of the time that was never discussed. It happened during the Depression, so the cause was probably financial, but no one seemed to know for sure. It must have been pure hell for my father, and it explained a lot of his anger. He wanted to put it behind him, I'm sure, but his deafening silence about it made us live with it all the time.' Armistead, in fact, spent his adolescence worrying that suicidal tendencies might be hereditary and keeping a nervous eye on his volatile father who was known to keep a captured Japanese pistol in his wardrobe.

But there were other, less morbid, outlets for his imagination. He had long since discovered the consolation of fiction and devoured *The Hardy Boys* and Robert Louis Stevenson with undiscriminating hunger. Reading, in turn, fed into his games. A best friend, Clark Crampton, used to join him on creepy expeditions crawling under the floorboards of Christ Church, the Gothic Revival pile the family attended in downtown Raleigh. Word had it that the first bishop of the diocese was buried under the altar, so the building was the closest approximation the boys could find to a haunted castle. Fired up by a book of North Carolina ghost stories, they also visited a stretch of coastal swamp railroad reputed to be haunted by the Ghost of Maco Station. Sure enough, way out in the dark, they made out the light said to come from a swinging lantern carried by the poor soul a train had decapitated. 'I'd never seen anything so eerie in my life. There was no rational explanation except cars rounding a bend somewhere and hitting the track maybe. But there it was. I remember breaking into a run thinking it was coming after us.'

An apt pupil, Armistead was spoon-fed the family tradition of ancestor worship, learning of a supposed kinship to the Royal Stuart line – an ancestor was one of many women claiming to have been impregnated by Bonnie Prince Charlie on his flight from Scotland – and that one branch of the family tree could be traced all the way back to someone called Siegfried the Dane. Armistead fell in love with a highly romanticized view of history, a process helped by there being a memorial to his Confederate general great-grandfather in the town square. 'I loved the sense of tradition and antiquity that I felt growing up in the South. I completely bought the whole Civil War mythology and the kind of phoney antebellum romance that was being peddled in *Gone With the Wind*. I was a little bit disappointed that that L-shaped ranch house of ours didn't have columns but it wasn't too hard to look at our maid and imagine her as Mammy. I grew up steeped in that lore and I was always grateful for it because it did have some colour to it.' He came to know Oakwood Cemetery by heart, where to find the tomb of the Indian Princess and so on, less from morbidity than a proprietorial sense of the past.

There was more history on family holidays. These usually involved long drives with the three children bouncing on a mattress in the back of the Country Squire. When not taking swipes at his battling brood or singing sea shanties at the top of his lungs, Armistead Sr would insist on making each cross-country voyage that much longer by leaving the road to follow the grey 'historical markers' to various graveyards and battlefields. Armistead's chief pleasures on such drives were the Burmashave signs – which doled out a limerick on a succession of little posts – and kitsch roadside attractions. Cherished among his memories of the latter are the Mystery Houses – buildings built out of kilter so that a mere child could look eight feet tall inside them – and a cunningly marketed optical illusion in New Brunswick called Magnetic Hill. 'It looked like you were driving down the hill into a mild valley and you would release the handbrake and you'd appear to be rolling back up the hill. It had to do with the configuration of the trees and the electric poles on either side of the road.'

As soon as he had freedom to go out alone and pocket money to spend in the local fleapit, a lifelong habit of film-going began to compete with his compulsion to read. 'I went off to see *Psycho* and *La Dolce Vita* at sixteen and they taught me all I needed to know about the world!' Don't shower without locking the door, stay clear of big-breasted women in fountains and invite lots of different people to your parties, presumably. 'I remember in particular the effeminate son of that aristocratic family in *La Dolce Vita* who's seen periodically dragging the cocktails along the floor on a little mobile cart and feeling "That could be me!"'

Armistead and his brother Tony had been playmates and co-conspirators as children. 'We dug holes in the backyard and connected them with an old hose so we could talk to each other. And we would ride the cable car for hours – this swing-like contraption my father built that would send us hurtling down the hill until we crashed into a tree. I loved the little whinny of delight that Tony would give whenever something made him happy.' But as adolescence approached and Tony grew into the model of a butch Maupin, destined for the Army, he and Armistead had less in common. Jane, was another matter. Armistead was constantly planning her career for her. For a long time he intended her to be a nun until she turned thirteen and grew breasts, whereupon he decided that she should be a supermodel, rechristened her Erika Thane and gained vicarious thrills mapping out the swath she would cut through society.

Along with films and books, a boyhood obsession which lingered on into adult life was with antiques. Egged on by his mother, who was herself an inveterate junk-store browser, Armistead even asked for antiques on his Christmas wish list at fourteen. ('How could my folks not have suspected *something?*') This in turn bled into an interest in interiors, beginning with his actually commissioning a stained glass window for his bedroom. 'The only place in Raleigh I could find to do it was an old man out in the country in a shed who did it for Baptist churches.'

Speaking about his youth now, Armistead conjures the image of a profoundly imaginative boy in a deeply unimaginative corner of the world. The lenses of his memory are not rose tinted. 'I was growing up in a fundamentally very bland time in a relatively suburban neighbourhood and I was wringing every drop of romance out of it that I could.'

College years

Towards the end of high school, Armistead was surprised to discover he could be popular. He had felt that his athletic deficiency and his signal failure to date would make him a complete outsider, someone who would never be elected to office or part of the in crowd. Then he began to see how he might establish a public personality for himself based on a reputation for wit. He played the town crier at something called the Queen of Hearts Ball, which involved parading around in a powdered wig and announcing the arrival of each girl, and found he could bring the house down during a weather emergency merely by stepping up to the microphone to announce, 'It raineth outside'.

At the same time, in league with his old friend Clark, he was becoming active in local politics, helping his father manage the campaign of a gubernatorial candidate. The boys painted a sign for said candidate on a huge sheet of plastic which they hung on the front of the Wake County Courthouse certain it was the largest ever made. The candidate proved unsuccessful but Armistead had acquired a taste for conservative political theory. Possibly to compensate for the social unacceptability of the sexual urges he could neither ignore nor dare act upon, he was growing into a deeply reactionary young man. 'It was such an extreme form of conservatism that even my friends found it vaguely unnatural. But I realized I could do two things with it. I could make a name for myself and I could please my father.'

It was decided that as a preparation for studying law, Armistead should proceed to the University of North Carolina at Chapel Hill. In a letter to her mother, Diana explained that she felt the university 'is just right for Teddy. He's more of an individualist and they have Beatnik types there who walk around with their shirt-tails out.' Tony, meanwhile, needed discipline and structure, it was felt, so he was packed off to the Citadel. This was the notoriously rigid military college which only recently admitted its first woman and proceeded to humiliate her.

It was not quite the first time Armistead had left home. There were the three or four miserable trips to summer camp and when he was seventeen, in his last year at high school, he had been sent to Chapel Hill by way of a taster for college life, for something called Boys State, which wasn't half so exciting as it sounds. 'Bill Clinton did this at roughly the same time. Outstanding students from all over the state come and participate in a kind of governmental experience and elect officials and live together in dorms. I hated it so much that I thought I was going slightly insane. I couldn't wait to get home and be with my parents. And I kept asking myself what was it going to be like when I grew up. I remember thinking that I would buy the little house next door and that way they would always be near.' His staggering lack of independence was rooted in fear of the unknown, certainly, but possibly there was also another unspoken fear behind it, of what he might become if he dared stay away long enough for the parental inoculation against unrespectability to lose its potency.

Homesickness aside, Armistead Maupin was a model student. Socially at least. He made friends. He was elected vice president of the senior class. He was elected to every major honorary on campus, including one called the Order of the Golden Fleece, the latter being a major triumph in his eyes solely on account of the sexy initiation ceremony. 'You were seated in a darkened auditorium while *The Ride of the Valkyries* was playing and these tall, hooded, male figures would roam the aisle and suddenly lunge and grab you by the shoulders and pull you up to indicate that you'd been chosen ... And we were taken out into the woods and led around blindfolded with a bunch of other guys. Heaven! The person behind you had to have his hands on your shoulder and you had to have your hands on the shoulder of the guy in front of you. You sort of had to be there ...'

At high school he had dabbled in the school literary magazine. Drawn into student journalism at eighteen, he began to make a name for himself by writing a political column, 'A View from the Hill' in the college newspaper, the *Daily Tarheel.* His pieces were largely satirical but the intent behind them was in deadly earnest. 'I was drawing attention to myself by being a sort of Buckley conservative at a time when most of my contemporaries, even the casually racist ones, were fairly indifferent to politics.' One incident gives the perfect illustration of his stance. There was a greasy spoon on the edge of town which continued to deny access to black people. A group of black and white protesters conducted a sit-in at the establishment and the proprietor retaliated by removing her panties and peeing in the face of one of the protesting professors. Armistead wrote a column in this woman's defence. 'I was doing the same thing that homophobes do today, namely inventing other justifications for my bigotry. Homophobes say it's a question of religious principles rather than admit to the fear and loathing in their hearts. I was doing the same thing when I argued for this woman's right to conduct her business the way she wanted.' Segregation was as much a mental attitude as an imposition of physically restraining laws. 'It was quite commonplace for people to say "I like black people, as long as they know their place. We feel great affection towards Fill-in-the-Blank. She's like a member of our family. We'd do anything for her." All this was true but we also didn't have a clue as to what her life was about.'

In 1962, the far right in America had yet to forge its uneasy confederacy with religious fundamentalism. A firm line on racial segregation and socialism was touchstone enough for their campaigners. A corollary of this was the collision of religion and politics when the Civil Rights movement gained momentum. Led by Armistead Sr, the entire Maupin pew at Christ Church emptied in protest when a sermon was preached in praise of integration and Martin Luther King.

Besides his father, young Armistead's political mentor was an altogether cooler operator called Jesse Helms. Now a notoriously anti-gay (anti-Mapplethorpe) senator – described by Armistead as an omniphobe – he was then executive vice president of a Raleigh television station. Every night he would broadcast a five-minute editorial in which he railed against black radicals, communists and communist sympathizers. 'He wasn't that well known then. He was simply the local editorial person. But that's how he came to fame; because all these people in North Carolina felt the way he did and felt tremendously validated to have someone there putting a fairly sophisticated face on their fairly primitive feelings. He was one of the first people who really learned how to dance around the accusations of hatred and bigotry.'

Fired up by his enthusiasm for Helms, Armistead became the first member of the family to register as a Republican voter when he turned twenty-one. His parents and grandparents had all voted Democrat, as was the traditionalist Southern way until Barry Goldwater's breakthrough, Abe Lincoln having been a Republican ... Daring to vote Republican seems like a contradiction in terms now but in 1964 Armistead felt he had joined an exciting, new political movement. His family were proud. 'And I was acutely aware that they were proud and somewhat relieved because I'd already been hiding my gay feelings for seven or eight years. This was insurance against their disapproval.'

The college atmosphere was intensely heterosexual, however, so Armistead told his friend Clark he was saving himself for marriage, ('You could still do that then with a relatively straight face.'), though he did feel obliged to go on dates occasionally. At one point, working on the safety-in-numbers principle, he dated two sisters, 'good folks' who both bore the middle name Armistead. 'My parents were very happy that there might be this serious in-breeding going on – but if they were cousins, they were very distant, because we didn't know them. Both of them were rather pretty and I can remember taking one of them down to the woods on the outskirts of Chapel Hill after a big snowfall and standing with her on a bridge with this idyllic scene all around us and kissing her and feeling absolutely nothing. And feeling great despair that I felt absolutely nothing.'

In one respect, however, it seemed he could do as his parents wished. After four years of college, he stayed on at Chapel Hill, graduating to the law school. Until now his only real ambition had been to do something that involved speaking in public. The arts were rarely offered as an option on career day, the choices being largely restricted to Doctor, Lawyer, Banker or Engineer/Architect. (The church, apparently, was the unofficially acceptable option for closet cases. When news finally reached him that Armistead was gay, Armistead Sr's response was reportedly, 'Well why didn't he tell us earlier? We could have gotten him into the seminary!') Acting, even had it been on offer, was beyond the pale socially and lawyers got to perform and show off in a way. So law it was.

There was just one problem; Armistead's complete lack of interest or aptitude. Though he was somehow elected president of his freshman law class, he bluffed his way through with the aid of gouges, the legal equivalent of Brodie's Notes, and kept his sanity by sloping off regularly to watch double feature matinées downtown. At the end of the year, however, he cracked during an Equity exam. 'I was in complete denial about my hatred of the law, but it became more and more apparent to me as I sat at the cafeteria at lunch and looked at my fellow students and realized they were genuinely interested in what was going on. They would actually argue about the cases.' Whereas Armistead would rather have argued the finer points of Fellini versus Wilder. So he walked out of the exam, thumbed a lift back to Raleigh and dropped the bombshell. His father astonished him by accepting the news graciously and claiming that he only wanted Armistead in his firm for the pleasure of his company. 'He told me the law had always bored him a little and he thought I might make it more interesting. I don't think that was the truth, but it was a nice thing to say.'

While he pondered his next move, Armistead took a job offered by his then hero, Jesse Helms, at the TV station. He would occasionally be seen on air conducting interviews, usually just the side of his face as he held a microphone out to his subject. (This was the first of several experiences that would feed into his creation of a journalism career for *Tales* heroine, Mary Ann Singleton.) At that point his grandmother Mimi had become so infirm with Parkinson's disease and Alzheimer's that she'd been moved out to Mayview, the old people's home. She was duly told to watch out for her grandson on TV. She got so into it that after a while she started seeing other members of the family on the screen. One day when Armistead visited her she burst out, 'The nigras have killed your father! A mob of radical nigras. I saw it on TV.' She could not be convinced otherwise, Armistead said, 'until my father came out and lay down and held a lily over his chest like a dead man and finally made Mimi laugh. Laughing was something we all knew how to do.'

ARMISTEAD IN THE BLACK BERET OF THE RIVER PATROL FORCE, CHI LANG,
VIETNAM, 1969. HE CALLED THE MONKEY ASSBREATH. SHE DOTED ON
HIM NONETHELESS

In the Navy

Still characteristically keen to conform and appease following his flunking out of a law career, Armistead suggested he follow in Armistead Sr's pawprints and enlist as a naval officer. The Vietnam War was at its height in any case so if he didn't apply for officer candidate school he would almost certainly be drafted. His mother filled out the application form for him and handed it back for him to sign. The form requested applicants admit to the following diseases: TB, cancer, homosexuality ... 'It was, you know, check if you've ever had one of these.' The homosexuality box went duly unticked; in all honesty he could say at this point that he had never had a homosexual episode.

Rejection for military service was regarded as a greater shame than flunking law school and both parents were deeply afraid their boy would fail his medical on account of something they had dubbed 'a pigeon preener', a tiny oil gland at the base of his spine akin to one in birds. During World War II, people with these had found them so cruelly inflamed by bouncing around in Jeeps that they were said to be smitten with Jeep's disease. Happily a sympathetic Raleigh doctor was procured who knew how to stitch Armistead up so that the gland would pass undetected by a Navy medic.

Armistead was accepted for officer candidate school and completed his harsh formal training in Newport, Rhode Island. Rising at five daily, he was so exhausted and so terrified that he found, to his relief, that his libido shrivelled. At least temporarily. 'It was one of the few times in my adult life when I didn't feel any carnal desire whatsoever, when I thought I might not actually be gay. But it came roaring back after two weeks.' He was not a born officer but charm and instinct helped him survive. He learned to fake rifle drill but only just, not being one of Nature's drum majorettes: 'I've never had *that* particular queer gene. I'm not graceful in that way.' Most terrifying was a simulated sinking ship called the USS Buttercup on board which he had to stuff a mattress in a hole and survive on the last two inches of air.

Suitably for a man ushered into the world by semaphore, he passed on to communications school, still in Newport, and life improved. He rented one of the Vanderbilts' charming converted stables with four other young ensigns just half a mile from the Hamilton Fish House where *High Society* was filmed. Tooling past the big oceanfront mansions in his new racing green Sunbeam Alpine convertible, sporting navy whites, he lived out his own gay fantasy but now freely confesses it was 'All style and no substance'.

Armistead has always enjoyed the company of straight men and credits his time in the Navy as having made this easier. He made friendships during his time as an ensign which he maintained beyond his tours of duty and beyond his coming out. 'When I'm working with my British trainer at the gym, we'll play that little game of 'look at that girl over there'. He knows I'm queer. We talk about it all the time. We joke about it. But I do that as a sort of hands-across-the-sea gesture to him and he gets a big kick out of it. And I like being a man with other men. I love the notion that it's just our dicks and that we're fundamentally the same creature, just pointed in different directions. And the more I talk to straight guys, the more I realize there's some truth to that.'

In Newport, he learned his communications lessons parrot fashion, finding inductance, resistance and capacitance remained utterly incomprehensible. His first tour of duty was on a destroyer tender, the USS *Everglades*, based in South Carolina, from 30 June 1968 to 18 July 1969. Suddenly he was in the middle of a Tom of Finland fantasy. An ex-Navy tailor later told him that many of his gay clients would specifically ask for a sexier look. 'They wanted the pants tighter across their ass or tighter across their thighs to show off their baskets. So there was this little conspiracy to make some of the uniforms sexier. It wasn't just my imagination.'

Suddenly the torture wasn't that Ensign Maupin had to pass muster with a rifle but that he had to remain aloof in the midst of so much rampant homoeroticism. 'The straight guys all grabbed each other's asses and said, "Oh gimme a piece of that". They were horny as hell and they would say to each other, "Man, you walk by me one more time with that ass and you're gonna get it!"' Luckily the officer's uniforms weren't half so revealing as the men's. But Armistead was so terrified of having his true thoughts revealed that he avoided such horseplay at all costs.

Apart from a brief tour into the Mediterranean to Naples and Malta, most of his time was spent in the wildly romantic Deep South setting of Charleston. He rented a carriage house on the edge of the Battery, at the very tip of the Charleston peninsula where all the fine antebellum houses stand, settling with unerring instinct a stone's throw from the local cruising ground. Judy Garland's death and the raid on Greenwich Village's Stonewall Bar may have passed him by, ('Nobody heard about Stonewall, let's face it. That was a PR campaign after the fact ...) but his first homosexual experience, in the summer of '69, had all the potency of the Apollo moon-shot. 'I was sitting in the park, one of the most beautiful places in the world, in all innocence at not quite dead of night, watching the moonlight on the water. And a man, a sort of effeminate, not very attractive man, walked by, rather heavily scented, and said, "Have you got the time?" It was a total howdy-sailor routine. And I knew exactly what he was up to and said, "I'm not what you're looking for." And he left. And I sat there for another ten minutes and thought about it and finally said to myself, "I'm *exactly* what he's looking for!" And I went back and scoured the park and found him sitting on a bench chatting someone else up and I said, "I'd like to apologize for my behaviour back there and I was wondering if you'd like to come to my place for a drink." I thought that maybe I'd just discovered the only other queer in the World! I didn't want to let him go.'

Love did not bloom but Armistead did, despite his terror that the man had spotted his officer's cap on his dresser and would blackmail him. 'It was not that night that I felt like a new man but the next morning. I remember driving down to the ship in that Sunbeam Alpine and turning on the radio and the Neon Philharmonic was singing a song called 'Good Morning Girl' and the lyric was:

Good morning, Girl.
You're several ages older now.
So powder puff your pretty nose
And eat your box of Cheerios
And go out and find your man where the wild wind blows.
Good morning, Girl.

It spoke to me and after I got over the initial terror that my life had somehow changed and the letter H was branded on my forehead for all to see, it occurred to me that there might be cuter guys where that one came from.' Lust and curiosity overpowered his terror of detection and he plunged back to the park night after night, undeterred by a brush with the local police, who caught him in a car by the docks with a married man too drunk to drive, or by the sight of a sailor being piped ashore after a General Discharge for homosexuality. 'Charleston was such a sultry place. You felt sex oozing out of every corner of it.' And soon enough Armistead was feeling something else: a virulent itching in his groin that signalled his first case of crabs. 'I was horrified to discover they were actually little animals. I'd heard my men talk about "skivvy crickets" but I'd always thought crabs were a rash. And I was afraid to go to the medic, because I thought he might be able to tell the difference between gay crabs and straight crabs. Years later I would think about that again, and how silly it had sounded, when people started talking about a gay virus.'

When the captain of the *Everglades* was transferred to Saigon, Armistead asked to join him, and so, for his second tour of duty, served under Admiral Elmo Zumwalt, the head Navy honcho in Vietnam. 'My father was thrilled, since he'd always told me that every generation of men get their war, and this was obviously mine.' But as assistant protocol officer Armistead's chief duty involved organizing tours of the war for visiting dignitaries. The Admiral was liberal and stylish by Navy standards, as was his Shanghai-born wife, and seemed to dote on Armistead. Soon the young ensign found himself taking the boss' wife and other high-ranking military wives on shopping trips through Saigon; a sort of society walker, with a '45 strapped on him. The prize item on these trips was an oversized ceramic elephant, known among GIs as a Buffy, short for Big Ugly Fucking Elephant. His head still awash with Lawrence of Arabia fantasies, Armistead grew increasingly frustrated with his less than heroic job. 'There was something called a Combat Action Ribbon which you didn't get unless you'd been officially fired at. And I entertained fantasies that someone would take a snipe at me during one of those shopping trips ...'

At Armistead's request he was transfered to the boondocks, to an army camp on the Cambodian border, where he served as a naval liaison officer in the town of Chau Doc, on the edge of the muddy Bassac river. Here it felt more like a war. He sat every day in a sandbagged bunker, with three enlisted men under him, and tracked by radio the movement along the Vinh Te canal, thereby protecting Army from Navy, Navy from Army and civilians from both. It was a profoundly tedious job but there was fantasy-food aplenty. Shunning the mess hall, he would go as native as he dared, eating rice rolls and fish in some thatched-roof restaurant in town, pretending to have stepped out of a Somerset Maugham story. He had his own army Jeep, christened Olivia Drabbe, and wore his fatigues with elephant hide sandals. Without exactly declaring himself, he began to develop and celebrate his social difference. Notably, he became friendly with the Vietnamese soldiers who stood watch with him, disarmed by their easy, tactile affection. He noticed how other Americans would mock the Vietnamese sailors because when night fell and boats were tied up in the river and everyone was sleeping on deck, the Vietnamese slept spoon-style for the comfort and warmth. They also thought nothing of linking pinkies when walking down the street.

But sex was absolutely not on offer. At least nowhere that this still green queen could spot it. His thirst for fantasy, however, was regularly met at the Seabee hut, the ultra butch hangout of the army's construction brigade. Hut was a misnomer since the men had occupied a high arched terracotta building built in the 1890s by the French Foreign Legion. Films were screened here. Few were sent but Armistead devoured them all, including, repeatedly, *Gone With the Wind*. Bats in the room would fly towards the lit-up screen, lending a new, gothic quality to Tara.

Even moving closer to the battlefields and vomiting over Vietcong territory when he became airsick in an Air Force colleague's little plane had not dimmed Armistead's hunger for an authentic war experience. Neither had the distinctly *Apocalypse Now* sensation of water-skiing on the Mekong, trusting his pilot to know how to avoid flaying him alive on submerged barbed wire. On Christmas Eve he went out on the canal (having first decorated his boat's gun with a wreath) to watch helicopters fly overhead blaring out a distorted version of 'Silent Night' and shooting festive red and green flares which mingled with actual gunfire. There were firefights all along the canal and another sailor, aware of Armistead's blank combat record, wryly offered him a grenade to throw. Suddenly Armistead was back on a school playing field, reliving every nelly's nightmare of being asked to toss the jocks' ball back into play, and, sure enough, his throw fell short. 'I heard everyone around me going, "Shit!" and suddenly we were down frantically covering our heads.'

His innocence remained extraordinary. During his honorary induction into the Seabees on New Year's Eve, in which he and another young officer were blindfolded and encouraged to shred their shirts with an axe, he got into a wrestling match (as you do ...) with an officer who subsequently played him a bootleg tape recording of *Boys In The Band*, and showed him the text of Auden's 'A Day for a Lay' in *Avant Garde* ... and Armistead still managed to ignore the semaphore. 'I was so persuaded that my precious little secret had to be protected at all costs that I didn't see when other people were sending out signals.'

Towards the end of his tour Armistead had a chance to strike an heroic pose at least at his sister, Jane's wedding. His family hadn't expected him, of course, since this was war, but Armistead persuaded Admiral Zumwalt to send him home on a fake courier run, which involved merely visiting another admiral in Washington and saying, 'The wet bird only flies at night'. As a joke. At Raleigh/Durham Airport he changed into his most glamorous camouflage fatigues and black beret 'And of course I had constructed the whole thing to make it look like Noble Warrior Returning from the War. My father was mowing the lawn when he saw me, and he said 'Goddamn!'

in a loud voice and came running out to meet me, proud as he could be.'

Armistead and his father belong to an hereditary organization called the Society of the Cincinnati, which owns a spectacularly beautiful turn-of-the-century mansion on Embassy Row in Washington. Jane and her new husband spent the first two nights of their honeymoon there and Armistead stayed there on his way back to Vietnam. Not only was the mansion complete with mouldering tapestries, secret passageways, ballroom, clanky lift and an ancient black butler but, unbeknownst to Armistead, it was slap bang in the middle of Dupont Circle, Washington's cruising area. Alone, disoriented by his brief trip home, suddenly worried that he might actually be killed with only a few weeks to go, he wandered out into the circle and instantly sensed the sexual energy there. 'And there was a very tall, all-American basketball player kind of guy that I started talking to. I didn't know what the protocol was, or anything else, and I ended up offering this guy money if he would come back to my place. There was nothing he said to me or did, nothing spectacular about the sex. But it was just the fact of him that got to me - so much so that I pined for him as I flew back to Vietnam. To this day, I can't hear Karen Carpenter singing 'Close To You' without thinking of him.' It was, too, a profoundly symbolic gesture for Armistead; leading somebody from what still seemed like a gay underworld into a building so symbolic of the family's values and making love with him down the hall from where his sister had so recently had legally and ecclesiastically blessed sex with her husband.

Processing out of the Navy in 1970, on Treasure Island, the site of San Francisco's 1939 World's Fair, he had his first prolonged sight of the city that would become so famously his home, but he was too disturbed by the upheaval in his life to take the place in. His tour of duty was up and he was free to leave but he had felt a profound security in playing an agreeable eunuch in the all-male company. He could have stayed on but knew that sooner or later his libido would land him in trouble. 'It's one thing to be secretly queer and a junior officer who gets to goof around and not take things seriously. But if you stick around and decide to make it a career, you want to think about advancement and all of that and I simply knew it wasn't going to fit with who I was. But I felt a real sense of melancholy. I can still remember being out on that island and thinking, "Maybe you should stay. This might be a mistake. You feel comfortable here."' The Navy, of course, was a time-honoured refuge for closet cases. 'It was absolutely wonderful in that regard. The obsessional opportunities were tremendous!'

Nixon and co.

Fleeing the glimpses of bourgeois hippiedom San Francisco had granted him, Armistead returned to the reassurances of the familiar South and a job on its oldest daily newspaper, the *Charleston News and Courier*. His speciality was vivid Southern stories with a Gothic edge – the nearby chitlin festival, A Spanish moss blight, an exposé of a local house claiming to be the film location of Tara. He soon teetered out of the closet to a trusted straight colleague, 'Because I wanted *somebody* to be a witness to my life.'

He had barely begun life as a journalist, however, when a friend from Admiral Zumwalt's office in Saigon, now working for Nixon at the White House, extended an invitation. Would Armistead like to return to Vietnam to work on a civilian project with other ex-GIs? Armistead jumped at the offer. He was missing the Vietnamese landscape but also he was missing the company of men, the camaraderie, the late-night talks. Such were still his politics at this stage that his interest in the project grew keener when he found it was part of a right wing propaganda offensive. His friend worked for Chuck Colson, a member of Nixon's infamous 'dirty tricks department'. They were mounting a campaign to prove that some American GIs supported Nixon's efforts in Vietnam in a counteroffensive against the Vietnam Veterans Against the War. Filled with righteous ire against Hanoi Jane (as Jane Fonda was then dubbed) and her pinko cohorts, Armistead regarded the venture as a patriotic duty. The idea was to return to the Mekong delta, live in a village and build houses for disabled Vietnamese veterans.

Armistead came to Washington and, using veterans' organizations, assembled a group of ten ex-GIs. 'So we went to live in this village called Cat Lai, outside of Saigon on the edge of a rice paddy. And there was this half-constructed cinderblock, motel-style building that we helped put the roof on.

I mean, we did *very* little construction, to tell you the truth. And at the end of it all reporters were unleashed to interview us about our efforts on behalf of the Vietnamese people. It wasn't cynical on our part. We believed in what we were doing. But I know now the whole project was *thoroughly* suspect.' One of a number of sceptical journalists who came to interview the workers on the oh so hiply named Cat Lai Commune, was Gloria Emerson. Armistead parried her questions as best he could and remembered her name – one that would surface again when Tricky Dick himself praised him for his efforts.

Armistead was halfway to San Francisco, bound for a brand new life in his Opel GT, when word came that he and his fellow communards were wanted for a half-hour audience with the President in the Oval Office. Nixon, Armistead recalls, was profoundly uncomfortable being with a group of young men. He remembers the sweat on the President's upper lip, and the excruciating sound of him trying to pass muster as a lad, purring, 'Oh don't you love those little Vietnamese girls; the way they look on their bicycles with those long dresses flowing out behind them. Like little butterflies!' In order to curry favour, Armistead told Nixon he had been grilled by a liberal reporter who had attempted to prove that he had returned to Vietnam in order to atone for some atrocity he had committed there. Rather than merely shrug it off as a commonplace, Nixon narrowed his eyes and asked, 'What was her name?' repeating the question when Armistead blustered politely. Told finally, he murmured, 'Gloria Emerson is a *total bitch*.' (Which Emerson delighted in hearing when Armistead told her about it years later.) The Veterans' Administration handed out plaques and autographed pictures of each fine young thing shaking the President's hand (providing at least one of them with spooky loo decoration for years to come.)

Armistead was subsequently invited to participate in the '72 Presidential inauguration. He sat with Nixon and Mamie Eisenhower at the deeply creepy 'inaugural youth concert'. 'They had a Republican almost-heavy metal band there that was singing a song called 'If You Don't Want My Peaches, Don't Shake My Tree' and Mamie had these two little gloved fingers stuck in her ears. And David Eisenhower and Tricia were sitting there. And Pat, of course.' At one point the audience was required to clap along and

Armistead noticed that Nixon, already wretched amid his gamely toe-tapping family, was the only person in the entire room who failed to find the beat.

The Watergate scandal broke during Armistead's early days in San Francisco, breached, naturally, by two heroic journalists. He did not reject his right wing philosophy overnight. Rather, it suffered a slow process of attrition in a city where no one approved of Nixon and where the counterculture held sway. Principally it was sex that brought him to transfer his allegiances. The orgy room at Dave's Baths was democracy made flesh; race and social standing were checked at the door along with clothes. Not, however, one's mobile closet; Armistead continued to sign himself in as Elloughby Branch – a joke on his Confederate general grandpa, L.O'B. Branch.

His experiences in the Navy and in Vietnam had begun to shake his racism, however, and San Francisco continued the process. 'Even here there's a tendency for gay life to be white and middle class, but I began to recognize the nature of prejudice. I mean, I'd passed beyond the pale when I became a full fledged fag and I realized there were a lot of people that hated me unreasonably simply because of that. And I began to realize that that must be true for black people as well.' He had often thought the prejudice against gay people was directly proportionate to the degree to which we were able to be invisible. He had been a party to the arguments used by Southern racists – that blacks were less than human because they lived in squalor and didn't work – used to justify keeping them in grinding poverty and excluding them from jobs. Now he saw this was akin to the argument barring gay people from legal recognition of their relationships on account of their lack of social stability. 'You're not like us so we're not going to *let* you be like us!'

Back in the early Seventies however he was still happy to write a piece for *National Review* about the Cat Lai Commune and the wholesome young men who didn't think war in Vietnam was evil, and thrilled to bits by a letter from editor Bill Buckley's sister saying that Bill loved the article in question. He was still hanging the picture of him and Nixon and his invitation to the inaugural ball on his apartment wall with no sense of irony despite the fact that many of the men he took home reacted as if they'd walked into Jeffrey

Dahmer's lair. It was a period when it was assumed that if you were out of the closet you had to be left wing. As late as 1974, when Armistead agreed to be the one gay person listed in a (very local) feature called 'The Ten Sexiest Men in Town', the piece read, 'Maupin, who is homosexual, does not consider himself an activist: "Who wants to make a career out of being oppressed," he says.'

When the time did come to consider himself an activist, he did not undergo such a complete conversion as to forget how deeply he had once cherished his conservative views. However unhinged they might seem, he knew never to underestimate the enemy's deeply held beliefs as mere malicious posturing.

The front page

Romantic and Southern though it might be, Charleston was too small for Armistead and he didn't want to spend the rest of his life waiting for sex in a parked car down on the Battery. He was rescued by Holger Jensen, an eminent Associated Press journalist who interviewed him at the Cat Lai Commune. When asked, Jensen offered him an interview. 'So I went to New York and they put me in a glass booth and gave me all the particulars of Lucille Ball's latest wedding to someone called Gary Morton. And I had to put it into a viable AP story, which I did, making reference to a zany redhead in the first paragraph.' On the basis of this alone, Armistead was offered a job at the AP's Buffalo bureau but turned it down, having been warned Buffalo was the last place off to which any self-respecting young closet case would want to shuffle. Two days later an opening came up in San Francisco.

The tyro reporter piled all his worldly wealth into his car and began the 3000-mile drive to the City by the Bay. Besides that detour to The White House, the most memorable aspect of the trip was a snowbound motel in Laramie, Wyoming – a town made notorious in 1998 when a young man named Matthew Shepard was tied to a fence and beaten to death for being gay. But Armistead will never forget the place because of a young blond desk clerk who watched *Death Takes a Holiday* with him on TV before making him more than usually welcome. He remembers that as the exhilarating start of his new life; a realization that the world was full of possibilities, even stuck in the snow in the middle of nowhere.

On one of his last nights in Charleston, he had told someone where he was moving. 'And he said, "Ooh, you'll love it there. They've got *fifty* gay bars there!" And I said rather grandly, "I'd never go in one of *those*." And I was in one of *those* the night I got in. The very night.'

Northern California was then such a hotbed of radical politics that even the AP bureau was affected. Armistead's recent meeting with Nixon, which had delayed his arrival at the bureau, was taken as a dubious reference indeed. By way of punishment, his first assignment was to cover a mercilessly long peace march in Golden Gate Park. Politics aside, he was a hopeless agency writer. News agencies require news-writing machines, constantly on deadline, constantly updating their text. The last thing they need is character. Armistead became swiftly demoralized, flinching every time the subs watered down his prose. 'I wanted to show off and you don't even get a by-line in the AP. The one story I can remember doing and liking was the night I was sent to the East Bay to write a story about the gypsy community there and I ended up meeting the local king of the gypsies and writing a colourful piece about it. But I spent far too long on it because I wanted it to be witty.'

There were compensations however. He settled in an apartment on Lafayette Park, a popular cruising ground, acquired a mynah bird called Sam and a best friend, an actress called Nancy McDoniel. Nancy played Nurse Ratchet in the local production of *One Flew Over the Cuckoo's Nest* and is acknowledged by Armistead as the first prototype for his *Tales* heroine Mary Ann Singleton. Disaster struck, however, only six weeks into his new life when he came down with hepatitis, doubtless picked up in Lafayette Park. 'It was made all the more grim by the fact that I would return to the apartment, really dragging my ass, and pissing something that looked like bourbon, and this bird would be going, "How are ya? How are ya?"' He was so ill, he was forced to return to Raleigh and his parent's deafening lack of curiosity as to how he fell prey to the virus. 'All I would do was watch TV with them and when *Streets of San Francisco* came on I would say, 'That's two blocks from my house!' I was so filled with pride at this new place that was all mine.'

A hot apartment

At any time of year, clutches of hapless Barbaryphiles can be found traipsing around San Francisco's Russian Hill with a street map in their hands and a look at once determined and suspicious on their faces, convinced that even if Mrs Madrigal's a modern myth, Barbary Lane must be tucked away somewhere ... Houses and apartments resonate with such an almost Jungian force through both Armistead's life and his writing that I considered using them as the structure on which to hang this narrative.

After moving to San Francisco he was restless in his search for a home. Disproving Mona's Law – that you can have a hot apartment, a hot lover or a hot job but never all three at the same time – would come later; for now he'd have been happy with just one of them. In the period between catching hepatitis in Lafayette Park and hitting pay dirt at the *Chronicle* he moved frequently, living mostly on Russian and Telegraph Hills. He lived on the Filbert Steps at several locations. The address with the greatest resonance for *Tales* readers was 1138 1/2 Union Street where he stayed for three years and which he rented again for a while later on. Immortalized as Brian's bachelor heaven on the top of 28 Barbary Lane, it was a tiny apartment perched on a roof, variously nicknamed the Pentshack and Little Cat Feet – after the Carl Sandberg line, 'The fog comes in on little cat feet'. It was his first proper home in the city.

In 1976, when *Tales* began to make him a local celebrity, he was back in Little Cat Feet but he felt the need for space and some visible sign of his new life and grown-up salary. So he took on the building still known as the Duck House because of its murals, on Alta Street, overlooking the Filbert Steps. Eleanor Roosevelt was said to have stayed there with one of her girlfriends during World War II and Armistead says he was thrilled by 'the thought of all that celebrity pussy-bumping that was going on in my bedroom.' The Duck House was too large for him to rent on his own, salary or no, so he acquired a succession of room mates who, together with the gay couple in the flat downstairs, Ken Maley and Daniel Detorie, formed his first alternative family, the dedicatees of the first two books. 'It was a truly exhilarating time. Harvey Milk was still alive and AIDS hadn't happened yet and we were young and randy and conscious of being part of a revolution that was rooted in our honesty. Reporters would come to the Duck House from all over just to study fags in their natural habitat.'

In 1981 he moved into a bijou cottage at 655 $^1/_2$ Noe Street on Noe Hill and proceeded to raise unexpected laughs when he told English audiences, in all innocence, that he lived 'in a little cottage above the Castro'. He was joined there by Terry and by a red poodle he'd acquired from another customer visiting his dope dealer. (Originally named KY, the dog was promptly rechristened as the more dignified Willie.) When they needed breathing room, the threesome moved on up to a walk-up penthouse, complete with a mini steam room, on 2 Fair Oaks Street.

Earthquakes or no, San Francisco prides itself on having some of the most costly real estate in America and remains a city, like New York or Paris, where the majority remain lifelong tenants. It was only with the extra revenue brought from the first miniseries and the consequent book sales boom that Armistead and Terry were able to buy and create their dream home, where Armistead still lives. Perched high above the city, it's a cross between a boat and 28 Barbary Lane. The walls are clad in cedar shingles and there are wooden decks front and back, a porch that cries out for a rocking chair and a dog and, nestling in the subtropical garden to the rear, a nod to Marin County in the shape of a hot tub. It's not a fortress – there are no security cameras and it's perfectly visible from the street – but it feels utterly aloof from the bustle of the streets below; the perfect, sunny, writerly retreat.

Crappy little jobs

Armistead escaped back to San Francisco as soon as he had recovered from his hepatitis but left the Associated Press six weeks later, naively believing that with a college degree and some journalistic experience he could saunter into a job on the *Chronicle*. There followed one of those periods where it seems that nothing you are doing is leading anywhere, until you become a writer, when suddenly it all starts to look like raw material.

He sold reams of Thai silk to Pacific Heights matrons in a shop on Union Street called Fabulous Things. Not a success – Armistead is not a swatch queen. He worked for Kelly Girl but couldn't type fast enough so found himself unloading mannequins in a warehouse with a man like Steinbeck's Lenny, who kept squeezing their tits and laughing maniacally. He cross-checked computer printouts. He handed out fliers – surely the world's most reviled job after squirting scent at shoppers.

He also wrote letters for an Episcopal minister and manned said cleric's doomed crisis switchboard, The Fish Line, which, unlike Mary Ann's, no one ever rang. 'He ran this stylish little Craftsman church down in Cow Hollow. He was a very handsome, Robert Redford-looking guy with a wife and kids. And I came in rather proud of myself one day, because he was such a big liberal so I was sure he would understand, to tell him that I had been chosen as one of the "Ten Sexiest Men in Town".' Armistead added that the piece would mention that he was gay and name the church where he worked. His employer promptly turned white, shut the door and confessed that, because he was gay too, he would have to fire him. After this crucial early experience of own-team oppression, it was with some satisfaction that Armistead imagined the priest's embarrassment when his own curate, inspired by Armistead's example, subsequently chose to come out in the course of a sermon. This left the priest, still firmly closeted, in the weird position of chat show hostess Rosie O'Donnell forced into a public congratulation of Ellen DeGeneres for her honesty.

Armistead then tried, briefly, to work for an agency that handled the PR for the San Mateo County Convention Visitor's Bureau, 'which was a dreadful job because there's nothing in San Mateo County for visitors except the airport.' One day the photography studio across the hall talked him into replacing the absent model for a frozen pineapple advert they were shooting. It took five shots of bourbon to loosen him up. The ad – 'Out of the freezer and onto your spoon' – duly went out as a flyer in magazines, and Armistead mailed a copy to his parents in distant Raleigh. Fired up by such glamour, he then signed up as mail boy to an ad agency called Hoefer, Dietrich and Brown, partly because he liked their newly converted nineteenth-century building, but also to indulge in his Robert Morse fantasies.

'I had grown up with the Rock Hudson/Doris Day movies and *How to Succeed in Business Without Really Trying* and a number of movies where the bright young thing who worked in the mail room revealed his genius to all.' The agency became the model for Halcyon Communications and, just like Mary Ann Singleton, Armistead was expected to hang the flag on the front of the building every morning. It was there he encountered the copywriter who was an inspiration for Mona Ramsey. (She wore granny glasses and peasant dresses, had *Playgirl* centrefolds on her office wall and hookah pipes and was known as the Resident Freak. She was deeply flattered when *Tales* first came out and, spotting the resemblance between her and the feisty character, bragged to all and sundry ... then wished she hadn't when Mona turned out to be a lesbian.)

With no intention of *staying* a mail boy, Armistead wrote an office newsletter full, on his own admission, of forced witticism, which he disseminated with the mail. He was summoned to the chief executive's office, all gingered up because he was sure that, Hollywood style, they had spotted his talent and would offer him a contract. In fact they told him he had far too much ambition for the job and fired him. A suggestion he had made to one of the creative heads, that a bank loan be promoted with an image of dollars shaped into a car titled The 1974 Fastbuck, appeared soon afterwards in Hibernia Banks all over town.

Chastened, Armistead took a job as an account executive in a smaller agency, Lowry Russom and Leeper, where he would at least be paid to write copy. He decorated his office with his ancestral portraits and set about trying, and failing, to work up an enthusiasm for aluminium honeycomb and anti-wind canine suppositories. The latter depressed him so much, he came out to his boss by way of explaining the personal turmoil that was preventing him giving his creative all. The boss merely replied, 'Yuh. *And?*', which was an unthinkable response, then capped Armistead's confession by revealing that *he* was holding down his job despite adulterously humping the Swedish receptionist. Coming out, evidently, was beginning to lose its power. In his early days in the city it had lifted his spirits so much that he became addicted to it and would come out to cab drivers and strangers on the street. 'That's what I was attempting there; one more little catharsis to make me feel better about this boring job.'

Armistead not only quit, but committed himself to a purely creative career by having little cards printed up. They gave his phone number and announced, to anyone who would listen: *Armistead Maupin writes for a living.*

ARMISTEAD BY DAVID HOCKNEY, 1989, OIL ON CANVAS

Serial addiction

Having turned his back proudly on advertising, Armistead proceeded to starve all over again. He was caught in a dilemma. He needed to work to stay in the city he had fallen in love with but the only work available consisted of soul-robbing nine-to-five jobs and fluorescent lighting. In a strange way, writers need to *come out* as writers in order to avoid the deadening sense of leading a split life in which most of their energies are devoted to work that means nothing to them. 'Now,' he agrees, 'I feel like a completely different breed than the people who ask me what I'm doing this weekend. Because I'm usually not even aware that the weekend is coming up.'

Determined, he began to write magazine pieces and send them to local publications, like *Coast Magazine* and the *Pacific Sun*. It was the latter, a weekly newspaper based in Marin County, that unwittingly set him on the road to becoming a novelist. Launching a San Francisco edition, the editors needed a writer to provide some city colour. Armistead duly began to write chatty, one-page pieces in which he talked to the likes of a nude encounter girl or Rudi Gernreich, founder member of the Mattachine Society, America's very first homophile organization and inventor of that unworn *succès de scandale*, the topless swimsuit ... In his quest for a fresh story, he followed a lead a straight woman friend gave him about the hetero cruising scene at the Marina Safeway. 'They call it Social Safeway,' she told him. 'If you go down there you'll see that it's full of single people pushing almost empty shopping carts.' Everything she said was true but, finding it was impossible to make any of the shoppers admit why they were there, he invented a fictional character, sent her there and wrote about how she met the man of her dreams only to find *he* was with the man of his dreams. Her name was Mary Ann Singleton. The *Pacific Sun* editors were pleased and asked for a weekly follow-up. The page was named 'The Serial'.

Excited by this glamorous new opportunity and a shameless self-marketer even then, the budding author had little stickers printed announcing *The Serial by Armistead Maupin in the Pacific Sun* and walked up and down Polk Street, the gay district at that time, pasting them onto lampposts. Alas, the San Francisco edition of the *Pacific Sun* lasted only five weeks but after only five episodes readers were hooked. What was going to happen to young Michael Huxtable (as Mouse was first called), last seen entering a bathhouse? Armistead shelved the idea and had no plans to develop it further.

The *Pacific Sun*, meanwhile, hired Cyra McFadden to write a Marin County version, under the same title. She cast a cynical eye on her well-heeled, ex-hippie neighbours and produced what Armistead calls a 'peacock feather, hot tub, touchy-feely satire' that went on to become a national best-seller as a spiral-bound novel. This was hard for Armistead to swallow, not because McFadden had stolen any ideas of his – she hadn't – but because she should find such success at a time when his version, which by then had evolved into *Tales of the City*, was still considered too much part of the gay subculture to be commercial. Lesbian novelist, Rita Mae Brown wrote a piece for *Publisher's Weekly* making just this observation and concluding that it was Maupin's treating gay characters affectionately that placed his project beyond the pale. Maupin and McFadden became friendly, however, and once *Tales of the City* had taken off elsewhere, Armistead continued to keep Marin County out of the narrative, conceding it as McFadden's fictional territory.

Armistead continued to write freelance pieces for whoever would take them until 1975, when he caved in and finally took on a conventional, nine-to-five sort of job. At the San Francisco Opera ...

Nights at the opera

Armistead hated opera. Still does. But he loved theatre, he loved wigs. And scenery. And big women making lots of noise. The opera in San Francisco is a deeply entrenched part of the upmarket social season and he was not yet so far removed from his background for this aspect not to fascinate him even as it inspired his contempt. His parents were impressed, because it was the first steady job he'd landed since leaving the Associated Press, and carried the unmistakable whiff of grandeur. His job was to write a regular column called 'The Prompter's Box' for the city's performing arts magazine, in which he held forth about upcoming productions. As with aluminium honeycomb and canine wind-cheaters, he learned to bluff, mugging up from *Kobbé's Opera Guide* and international opera magazines. He learned to do it so well that he was bewildered to find himself arousing the interest of people obsessed with the subject even though he continued to retain as little knowledge as he had in radio communications classes.

His office was little more than a windowless opera house cubby-hole and he had to put up with the rampant homophobia of the artistic director, Maestro Kurt Herbert Adler who – nellyphobia notwithstanding – could remember all Leontyne Price's poodles by name. Armistead was also, unwittingly, collecting material for his later fiction, from both the hordes of A-gays prowling the premises and the bored society women hungry for useful cultural occupation. He became popular around the house by writing joke opera synopses featuring employees who were having a party or retiring. Largely thanks to these, and his wit at performing them, he landed a commission to write a new libretto, or more properly 'book', for a new, low budget production of Offenbach's operetta *La Périchole* for the spring season at the Curran Theatre. Seasoned librettist, Michael Feingold, had dropped out so Armistead was thrown into the new production at the last minute, Ruby

Keeler fashion, to come up with a spicy updating for the spoken dialogue. The original satirized goings-on at the Second Empire French court through a tale of a womanizing Peruvian viceroy, so Armistead swung the references around to target the newly publicized tales of President Kennedy's lechery in office. (A typical line was 'Ask not what your Viceroy can do for you but what you can do for your Viceroy!'). Armistead was in seventh heaven. Not only was the Curran Theatre a kind of gay shrine – it's where much of *All About Eve* was filmed – but the lead man was Leonard Frey, the actor who had created the part of Harold, the 'pockmarked Jew fairy' in *The Boys In The Band*. Frey's poised campery and Maupin's lines were well matched and the revival was glowingly reviewed.

Our hero's career in opera was short-lived, however, thanks to a phone call from a certain society columnist ...

Tales of the City

Charles McCabe was a stalwart of *The San Francisco Chronicle*. Not a typical Maupin fan, he was a crusty, homophobic, hard-drinking Irishman who wrote columns about shaving and smoking and his daily pilgrimages to Gino and Carlo's bar. The *Chronicle* was an Establishment newspaper, owned by the de Youngs (as in the museum) and famous for creating personality columnists like McCabe, Herb Caen and a notoriously misogynistic 'Count Marco'. At a cocktail party one evening, McCabe was holding forth about how he thought young Maupin's serial in the *Pacific Sun* was just the sort of 'vulgar crap' the *Chronicle* needed to attract a younger readership. He was overheard by the paper's society columnist, Virginia Westover, who did the decent thing and gave Armistead a call.

Armistead braved McCabe who took him to meet Charles de Young Thieriot, an editor famous for not giving a shit about the paper beyond dabbling in its society and hunting columns. Thieriot's approval carried the proviso that, because he was uneasy about fiction in a newspaper, the title had to reflect the fact that it was fiction and had to let the readers know that it was about San Francisco. The paper gave Armistead a list of proposed titles they would be happy with, San Francisco Stories and The San Francisco Story among them. *Tales of the City* was the one that jumped off the page however. 'It had a definite Dickensian ring to it.' He was hired and told to write six weeks' worth of column so they could have that much on credit, as it were, in case he ever fell sick. His first *Serial* character – wide-eyed out-of-towner Mary Ann Singleton was revived as the reader's way into both city and narrative. In true daytime soap opera tradition, a milieu was found where most of the characters, and therefore storylines, could believably run into one another. This was not a motel or a wool shop, however, but a charmingly funky lodging house run by a warm-hearted, all-seeing, dope-wielding

JANE AND ARMISTEAD WITH NEWSPAPER RACK, NORTH BEACH, 1981

landlady, Anna Madrigal. Michael Huxtable re-emerged as Michael Tolliver, the young, not especially handsome, not especially talented gay man who most readers fell in love with and came to regard as the serial's lead character. For all the serial's careful democracy, however, he did not appear until episode thirty-one apart from a fleeting appearance in the Social Safeway scene. Thirty episodes was six weeks' worth, and Armistead had decided to downplay *Tales'* gay content until he knew he could feel securely wedged in the paper's pages. Even more likely to prove offensive to the editors was Anna Madrigal's secret transsexuality, the hemp-scented bomb up Armistead's sleeve.

The managing editor who supervised *Tales* kept a chart in his office which had two columns. One listed each new heterosexual character as they appeared, the other, the other ones. He had yet to realize he was employing a screamer, Armistead having sat his job interview disguised in button-down Oxford and blue blazer, every inch Ensign Maupin of Raleigh, North Carolina. 'And the chart, of course, became more and more of a joke until I finally finished it off by writing an episode about Frannie Halcyon, the alcoholic society matron. It ran in the newspaper but it never made it into book form because everybody – my agent, my editor at Harper and Row, the newspaper editor – said it was in abysmal taste. And I look back and I'm so sorry I took it out because it was really funny.'

What happened was that Frannie came back from yet another liquid lunch and 'fell asleep' in the herb garden. Then her daughter, DeDe, returned to Halcyon Hill to find her mother deeply shaken and evidently a rape victim. She said, 'Mother this is 1976. Rape is not something you have to be ashamed of. Tell me. Who is it? Is it somebody we know? Is it Manuel the gardener? Who is it? Tell me!' Frannie continued to sob and wouldn't tell her. 'Mother,' DeDe insisted, 'This is ridiculous. You've got to come clean. Tell me what happened, at least.' So Frannie begins, 'Well I went to lunch with Vita and when I came back I took a stroll in the garden and I just lay down to have a little snooze. And when I woke up he was on top of me. And I just couldn't do anything about it.' And still she wouldn't tell her and when DeDe finally left the room exasperated, Frannie reached down to the Great Dane sleeping at her feet and scratched his ears and said, 'It's okay, Baby. Momma knows you didn't mean it ...'

When Armistead walked into the managing editor's office he found the man shaking his head. Armistead was adamant that the dog was going to qualify as heterosexual but his boss was not amused. 'He was a very sweet, kind of buttoned-down old guy who had an avuncular attitude towards me and was always saying, "What a shame. You know, there are a lot of cute girls out there that would really like you." But I had a semi-adversarial relationship with the editors for years. I had to fight for everything. Every new thing I did.'

When Armistead's first year's work – which we now know as *Tales of the City* – ended, he was met with a deafening silence from the *Chronicle*'s management. Then a colleague muttered, 'Follow me. I want you to see something,' and took him to a back room where three industrial-sized garbage cans were overflowing with fresh fan-mail from readers already suffering withdrawal from their daily dose of Maupin. Not knowing then what he learned later, Armistead was happy to be popular, made no move to hire an agent and remained content to be paid a basic reporter's salary. He was granted a fortnight's holiday then began work on the second year of instalments.

Tales of the City began running on 24 May, 1976. By the time the second serial started on Valentine's Day the following year, *Newsweek* and several major dailies had carried stories about it. There were also eight imitations in newspapers around the country including *Bagtime* by Bob Greene which ran in the *Chicago Tribune*. None succeeded. As with a television soap opera, what happened in the *Tales* column was set at the same time of year as when it would appear. 'Naturally, once the plot-lines started going, I couldn't always nail them into a specific time. But some events I was able to fix on as they happened.' The day after the Associated Press ran a story about Anita Bryant organizing her Save Our Children crusade in Florida, he had Mrs Tolliver write her preposterous letter to Michael about how thrilled she was about this wonderful new Christian campaign, not knowing her own son was gay. Few novelists can ever have been in a position to see their indignation fleshed out as public fiction almost overnight.

Meanwhile a *Tales* cult was building. *Chronicle* readers, eager for their friends outside the Bay Area not to miss out, began to photocopy the column, a week's worth at a time, and circulate it by post. (This was still the heady days before fax, let alone scanners and e-mail.) Before long Armistead was becoming known to his friends at the Duck House as the Xerox Dickens.

Come out, come out, wherever you are

Armistead had come out to a journalist in Charleston and then to his less than startled boss at Lowry Russom and Leeper, but he technically went public as a gay man in 1974 when he agreed to be listed as the lone gay on the 'Ten Sexiest Men in Town' list. That was less than courageous, however, because he knew his parents would never get to read it. He came out to them, in the *Chronicle*, by having Michael Tolliver write a coming out letter to his mother. He knew they were subscribing. In fact, they found out through *Newsweek*, when he agreed to be identified as a 'gay journalist' in a story on beauty queen - turned - homophobe, Anita Bryant. 'So I'm sure it was a little brutal. But in a way it was the kindest way I could do it because they didn't have to go through the big decision of whether or not they had to tell their friends.'

He can't stand it when I point out that this was also carrying on the family tradition of communicating by semaphore rather than face to face, just as his new novel, *The Night Listener*, will communicate thoughts on his relationship with his father that he cannot tell him in person. It's not a dialogue. It leaves no room for either parent to tell him how they feel, even to give him their blessing. Interestingly hundreds of gay readers of the *Chronicle* must have felt equally comfortable with such indirect communication because they chose to cut out the second year's episode titled 'Letter to Mama' and mail it to the unsuspecting folks back home with a 'me too' as a postscript.

Armistead Sr was the first to respond. Characteristically he wrote from the office, on a yellow legal pad so that the communication was somehow less disconcertingly intimate. By this stage Armistead's mother was very ill and Maupin pére implied that by putting her under emotional pressure, Armistead was hastening her death. He didn't write the word gay. He didn't acknowledge the contents of Armistead's revelation at all. What neither father nor son knew was that Diana had known her boy was gay for years thanks to a friend of his, and if anything besides her cancer was consuming her energy it was her effort to keep the knowledge secret from the husband she was sure it would destroy.

Edie Ridgeway was Armistead's last-ditch effort at heterosexual romance. Last-ditch doomed effort. She was a nice girl. He liked her. His parents liked her, Armistead Sr. because he could slap her butt and she took it like a man, Diana because it was like having another daughter around now that Jane had followed her husband to Germany. Armistead invited Edie on a visit when he first moved to San Francisco. He was having his first full blown love affair, with a lawyer named Philip Smith whom he describes as 'one of those preppy closet cases that thinks he's got a secret and *all* his friends know'. Armistead led poor Edie out to the tip of the pier in Aquatic Park, the point where Michael and Dr Jon (in *Tales*) have their first kiss. He hemmed and hawed and told her how very happy he was and she was utterly thrilled because she thought he was about to propose and then he finished his sentence and said that he was so happy because he had met this lawyer ...

Armistead poured a succession of Irish coffees down her at the Buena Vista bar to help her over the shock. The next day, while he was out at work, she popped some Valium and rang the friend who was not, after all, to be her mother-in-law and ran up a huge phone bill telling all. When Diana and Armistead Sr came on their first visit and, like Michael Tolliver's parents, endeavoured to 'help him settle in' at Little Cat Feet, Diana gave no sign of what she knew. They took him shopping for furniture in Marin and she kept saying, 'You could just get a single bed. You don't need a double. You won't have a wife for a long time.' Armistead Sr. meanwhile, blissfully oblivious, merely winked and said, 'I think you should get the bed you want, son ...' Back in Raleigh, hugging her poisonous secret, Diana took to poring over books on homosexuality in the library; not the big downtown one where friends might see and query her sudden interest in Kraft-Ebbing, Hirschfeld and Kinsey, but to an obscure suburban branch where she could hide in the stacks and study in peace. Her first reaction, once *Newsweek* and the *Chronicle* had brought it out in the open, was to tell Armistead, 'This is awfully hard on your father.' She subsequently told him, 'I just want you to be happy, darling,' and assumed the scandal would wreck his career. 'Mummie, you don't understand,' he told her. 'This *is* my career.'

In a sense, however, Armistead also had to come out to himself, not just to embrace his sexuality but to learn to celebrate it. The focal point for this moment was a strange trip, in every sense, made in the limbo period between delivering six weeks' worth of *Tales* to the *Chronicle* and hearing that they were prepared to commit to running it. A pick-up from the Lion Pub, a gay bar in Pacific Heights, rang up to say, 'I'm invited to an art gallery opening in Palm Springs and the names on the invitation are Rock Hudson and Prince Umberto Di Poliolo. [pause for effect.] Would you like to come?' Armistead jumped at the offer, eager for diversion. The art gallery was tacky and Rock Hudson didn't show up. However he fell in with Jack Coates, who had been Rock's lover for four or five years after Rock picked him up when he sold him petrol. What followed is best left to Armistead's narration.

'He was one of these sort of balding, bearded, unprepossessing-looking guys and then the clothes came off and he was just a sex machine. I went out to a little ranch house way in the middle of the desert with him and about twelve other guys and we all took something that was called TT1. I have no idea what the drug was. Amazes me that I just politely took it. I was told that it was a relaxant given to women in childbirth. It was the most extraordinary drug experience of my life. It was complete and utter going to heaven euphoria. It affected me so deeply I wrote a ten page letter to my sister that I've saved. Because so much happened all at the same time. I fell in love, briefly, with Jack Coates. Jack told me about a lover he had who was on the diving team in Berkeley. This nineteen year old, called Steve Del Re, came over to visit me subsequently at my little house on the roof. And I was smitten with him and the three of us decided that we were just perfect for each other. I must have gone slightly mad for six months or so but it was sort of a scouring brush that reached down inside of me and just got out every ounce of all the repressive crap that I'd ever been dealing with. And it was fabulous, you know? And that's when the writing started. That's when I knew I could write. The TT1 opened everything up ... Oh God. You know. Here's how strong it was. We were all basically kind of naked. It was an orgy but kind of a spiritual orgy

because it wasn't a great deal of screwing but there was a great deal of nakedness and wandering in the desert. I remember standing like this in the room and turning my head and it kept going and turning around and I saw everything in the room through 360 degrees. It was a beautiful place. Someone had a fox coat that was lined in satin and I remember putting it on at dawn and walking out into the desert and feeling so at one with everything. With nothing on but a fox coat.'

Rock and the hard place

A few weeks after the fur-coat-in-the-desert revelation, Jack Coates dragooned Armistead and the same clutch of friends over to the San Bernadino Playhouse to see Rock Hudson in a stage production of *John Brown's Body*. (This being 1976, Hudson was in his phase of trying to win credibility as a stage actor, which he would do most successfully as King Arthur in a touring revival of *Camelot*). Jack led them backstage after the performance. Armistead was one of the only men in the party not to have met Rock before; most of the others had at one stage been his pool boy, or his whatever. They got off to a fine start because they were no sooner shaking hands than a power failure plunged the dressing room into darkness. When Armistead murmured, clutching the big man's hand, 'Well this is the opportunity of a lifetime,' he was only half joking.

He knew he was in with a chance because it soon became clear that Rock was no chicken hawk but liked his men manly. During their second encounter, when Rock and his lover, Tom Clark, passed through San Francisco in late May, Rock invited the half-a-dozen young men he'd dined with at Mama's to join him for a night cap in the Diplomat Suite of the Fairmont Hotel. 'Rock already knew that the first episode of *Tales* would run in the *Chronicle* the next morning, so he secretly bought an early edition from the desk clerk and read it aloud to us up in the suite, rather drunkenly but with great charm.' This is the episode in which Mary Ann calls her mother and announces that she's not coming home to Cleveland. 'And it had extraordinary resonance for me of course because her mother says, "Oh are you sure you're going to be okay? Because there was somebody on *Macmillan and Wife* who was strangling secretaries ..." ', *Macmillan and Wife* being Rock's hit TV show. Later, as the group was leaving, Armistead was startled to see Rock jovially consider and reject Steve Del Re, the aforementioned pride of the Berkeley diving team, as too young. Then he invited Armistead to join him and Tom for dinner the following night. 'It was as if he'd been shopping.'

Dinner was at La Bourgogne, a stylish French restaurant at the end of an alley in the Tenderloin. Rock and Tom sat there tossing back Bullshots and even Armistead, who has always preferred dope to alcohol, became sufficiently plastered to offer to write the book about the star that would tell all. 'And his lover was the one who raised the biggest hue and cry, saying, "Not until my mother dies." And I remember thinking, "who in the world would hide Rock Hudson from his mother?" As it turned out, Rock had been talking about The Book for years and the running joke was, "Well, we'll save that for The Book."'

As the three of them began to weave their drunken way back up Nob Hill to The Fairmont, Tom Clark announced that he was too tired to walk and took a cab. Evidently this was part of a well established routine between the Star and his former PR man for leaving Rock alone with the latest, trembling young thing. This latest trembling young thing (thirty-two at the time) was in heaven. Rock had always been an icon of his and was not even slightly disappointing in the flesh 'He was a big man. He was completely and utterly charismatic. Rock was the perfect name for him. At fifty, his butt was solid. And he was very charming and looked you straight in the eye. And he was desperately in need of giving you exactly what you wanted to hear, to the point that he would try to pass himself off rather touchingly as being interested in gay rights whenever I was around him. Clearly he didn't have a clue about gay rights ...'

As they climbed the hill, Rock began jokingly thumbing rides from passing cable cars so that passengers started screaming, 'It's Rock Hudson! It's Rock Hudson!' They arrived in the Diplomat Suite to find that Tom Clark had passed out in the bedroom. Rock led the way to the living room, fixed them both another drink. 'We were both in suits and he sat across from me and we had a conversation for a while that was clearly about nothing to do with what was on our minds. And finally he said, "Well I should be over there or you should be over here," which I thought was about the sexiest thing I had ever heard anybody say. So I don't remember which one of us budged, but we did. And we had a sort of making out session, loosening ties and kissing. And we were finally rolling around on the floor when he said, "Hang on," and he produced a little black leather case that had R H embossed on it in gold. And he unzipped it and pulled out his poppers. He had a personalized Rock Hudson popper case! And I – just the way Michael did in the book – completely lost my hard-on. I was so overwhelmed at the notion that I was about to go to bed with Rock Hudson. Not to mention the fact that I'd just seen the baby's arm hanging between his legs. And we sat on the couch together and he put his arm around me and said, "You know I'm just another guy, like any other guy. You know that, don't you?" And all I could say to that was, "No. You're not. And I'm Doris Day." '

Rock playing the perfect gentleman paid off and the pair's later attempts were more successful. It wasn't a romance; they were becoming friends and sex was Hudson's chief way of expressing intimacy. But Rock's sexual adventurousness went hand in hand with a sentimental respect for the concept of a life partner. 'He thought everybody should have a lover. He was always asking me if I'd found one yet. So when I did meet somebody and this guy and I went off on a love boat cruise to Mexico, Rock insisted on meeting the ship in San Pedro. This was the cruise I wrote about in *More Tales*, where Mary Ann has her romance with Burke Andrew, which was just a clever rearrangement of my boyfriend's name. I remember Rock waving up at us from the dock when the ship came in. He was like a doting aunt or something, just tickled to death that I'd been off on a honeymoon. I didn't have the heart to tell him what a disaster it had been. The woman next to us at the rail totally lost it when she realized who was waving at us. I was so proud that he was my friend.'

But the restrictions of fame and the closet would ultimately cause that friendship to founder. 'Quite a lot of famous people become curiously passive about the people they know and accept. Their hangers-on just call them and say, 'I'm in town,' and their house becomes a sort of hotel. And I could have done that continually and lived off the residual glamour except that it wasn't very glamorous to be told that I would have to leave the house because Liz Taylor or Nancy Walker or somebody else he was playing bridge with was coming in the next day. As much as I liked Rock, I was just part of his sexual sub-life.'

The encounters with Rock and the graphic illustrations it gave of the workings and self-deception of the celebrity closet brought home to Armistead just how much he was growing in self-dignity as an out gay man. Having been a closet case himself only a few years earlier he suddenly found himself cast in the role of radical gay rights activist and he realized this would prevent their friendship ever developing beyond a superficial level. 'I started feeling my star was on the rise, so it was insulting to have to hide. I was building an identity for myself that was about telling the truth.' In effect, Armistead had become one of the first American celebrities to be gay for a living and he sensed that, for all the lip service he paid to The Book, Rock was never going to come out.

Rock continued to get in touch on the occasions when he passed through San Francisco and on one such occasion Armistead successfully dared him to come cruising. 'We started out at a disco and then we went to a South of Market leather bar called The Black And Blue that had a piece of corrugated iron hanging from chains with a sort of orgy room behind it in the little triangle that it formed. And he and I went back there and it was a lot of guys in black leather and Rock Hudson in a red alpaca sweater, looking like a tourist from the Midwest. Very tall, very handsome, but a slightly pot-bellied, stalwart, middle-aged man. And he stood there and nothing was happening. And I kept thinking, "If they only knew what they're missing!" And I was standing next to him and beginning to feel that it was slightly sad that he was a wallflower at a Hell Ball so I pinched his butt in a friendly kind of way and he said, "Is that you?" and I said, "Yeah," and he said, "Just checking." I'm now the age he was then, so I think I know what he was feeling that night, and it makes me feel closer to him.'

Armistead paid homage to his fading friendship with Rock in *Further Tales*, while taking a hefty swipe at closet Hollywood, by having Michael Tolliver link up with a closeted macho icon called _____ _____ , popularly known as

Blank Blank. There was no feedback from Rock about it – quite possibly he was not following the series – and Herb Caen was the only journalist who tried to spell it out, 'Think Brick Oldcar' was the way he put it. To this day Armistead insists he was trying to write about closeted stars as a breed, not Rock in particular. Had outing him been his intention, he would have dropped far heavier hints in the narrative. As it was, he changed details – substituting Mary Tyler Moore for Carol Burnett – that would have signposted Rock's identity too clearly. When *Tales* arrived in England the Rock story had yet to be broken in the press and I remember many male readers wondering hopefully if Blank Blank were James Garner.

Then Rock came back into his life with a vengeance when the news broke, after his withdrawal from *Dynasty* and suddenly haggard appearance on Doris Day's cable pet show, that the star had AIDS. A strange period ensued when the American media had no idea how to handle the story, whether to be saddened or scandalized, whether to play ball with Hudson's cronies and respect his privacy or tear the closet door off its creaking hinges. 'I think Mamie van Doren and I were the two people in America, because she had no career and I was completely out, who were able to speak of him affectionately and be comfortable about his homosexuality. There were just a handful of people who would take on that job of saying, "Yes. He's gay. He's very much loved. Everyone knew he was gay. The industry certainly knew he was gay. And don't you dare *sensationalize* this." '

Armistead's decision to go public had long roots. He had known since 1982 or so that the nature of his life was such that sooner or later he would have a moral obligation to tell the truth because of the standards he had publicly set for himself. 'There's really only one way to lift the stigma of homosexuality, which is to be matter-of-fact about it. So there was a very odd sense of the moment having arrived when this reporter from the *Chronicle* called me up and said, "You knew him. How do you feel about this?" And I basically said what a terrible tragedy it was that this nice man who had played this horrible game all his life was finally revealed through a deadly illness. And it became the source that was quoted in the rest of the press so they could justify their own discussion of his homosexuality.'

The weeks that followed were among the most stressful Armistead would ever experience. He was vilified in the gay press, especially the Bay Area *Reporter*, for what was seen as a betrayal of the home team. Outing had yet to be a word, even the concept was novel. 'The notion was that I was part of a secret fraternity and I had broken the rules of the fraternity.' Rock's sexuality was an open secret but one wasn't supposed to put it into words. 'The old queen who ran the sidewalk flower stand on Castro Street clucked his tongue at me as I went by. Jack Coates, the guy who brought Rock into my life, called up weeping and drunk one night and said, "How could you do that to that beautiful, beautiful man? How could you do it to him?" I knew that what I had done had come out of love and principle and in fact I had established a sort of template for the press that made things easier for Rock.'

It was a turning point in media coverage of gay issues and in particular of AIDS. A screen legend outed as having AIDS and as being gay; Hudson was tantamount to American royalty and the impact of the story, from the White House down, was massive. *People* magazine ran its first sophisticated piece about gay life, using material Armistead fed them. *Newsweek* and the rest followed. At that stage, however, gay lobbyists, anxious not to see research and care funding severed, were desperate not to have AIDS identified as a specifically gay phenomenon. Armistead received angry phone calls from interested parties insisting 'If we could have persuaded them he was straight then they would have done something about AIDS ...'

Meanwhile there were those still trying to 'in' the ailing star, even suggesting he had anorexia. 'That awful old queen, Ross Hunter, who produced so many of those movies, was quoted in the press as saying, "We don't know what the cause of it is. I've never known him to be homosexual." Ross Hunter used to go to orgies with Rock. He was lying in a big way.' And reporters pursued Armistead for quotes to say as much. He had never felt so alone in his life and the stress brought on such severe gastritis that he destroyed his stomach lining and persuaded himself that he had developed AIDS too. 'And in some weird way I felt guilt about it. I must say I felt guilt about it. I worried that I'd done something that had hurt him. I knew that morally what I had done was right in the general scheme of things but the thought that he was in pain somewhere and about to die and had perceived my motives as being wicked in some way was really painful to me. I finally forgave myself in a dream. I had this very eerie dream where he walked in like a ghost, very thin but quite beautiful, with luminescent skin, and stroked the side of my face and said, "It's okay, Buddy. It's okay." '

In fact Rock effectively sent this message shortly before his death by telling his biographer Sara Davidson that Armistead was the first person she should visit. By the time of his death in 1986 and the lurid scenes that accompanied it – the Pat Boones, for instance, trying to bring Jesus into his body at the eleventh hour – Rock had received some thirty-five thousand letters of support. A little late in the day, The Book *Rock Hudson; His Story* was to be written at last.

ARMISTEAD AND TERRY THE DAY AFTER THEY MET, ATLANTA, 1985 'I REMEMBER
THINKING IT WAS GOING TO BE A VERY IMPORTANT PICTURE'

Fighting the beast together

In 1985, dreadfully ill with gastritis, Armistead took the test for HIV. In the punitive fortnight's wait that followed, he convinced himself he was indeed infected, a process he now sees as guilty self-punishment for having outed Rock. While he was in this terrible frame of mind, vulnerable, filled with doubts, he received an invitation from someone at the Gay Student Alliance at Georgia State University to make an address there.

Terry Anderson was no gushing fan. As a part-time employee of Christopher's Kind bookshop, he knew of Armistead's books but hadn't read them. He had simply read an article in a recent issue of *The Advocate* in which, ironically enough, Armistead laid down some rules for how to be a happier homo. Read it and loved it so much that he photocopied it and circulated it. Terry was maddened that the queens in Atlanta spent all their time in bars and were completely apolitical. Characteristic of the scene there was the fact that the bars had back alley parking lots to enable closet cases to come and go discreetly. Terry toured the parking lots sticking Armistead's rules under every windscreen wiper. Then, after polling others about who could fill a theatre, it struck him that inviting Armistead to speak might both raise some money for the Gay Student Alliance and motivate the members. Armistead accepted the invitation and it changed his life.

The moment he saw Terry at the airport they clicked. 'I *liked* him at first sight. We were finding instant points of agreement, largely about the closet and movies, which are the two things that are most important to me! And I saw right away that he had really interesting judgements when it came to creative areas although he had not written a lot. It was such a relief to find someone who was as pissed off about the closet as I was, who understood my motives but was right alongside me in terms of understanding the concept of it all. And I was so relieved to be with him that I cried all over him. Part of those two days of falling in love was me just weeping in his arms.'

When Armistead first moved to San Francisco he had, like Michael Tolliver, a head full of romantic dreams of husky professionals with Labradors and a way with a power drill. 'My heart was breaking endlessly in the beginning because I was bringing these sort of fourteen year old girl standards to the world of Men! So I learned to get tougher about that. And I suppose I didn't realize to what degree a real love affair could tenderize my heart and make me reinstate some of those values.' He agreed with many of his peers that heterosexuals made a ridiculous fuss about monogamy and that most sex should be a form of recreation.

Meeting Terry changed all that. They talked frenetically all the way to the hotel with all the urgency of long-separated twins then grabbed each other and tumbled into bed, almost because the dialogue could go no further until they had. They then had the dilemma of trying to resemble a visiting lecturer and his earnest host for three days when in fact they were living off sex and room service. 'We went out only once, to a street fair, and we looked guilty as hell when we bumped into somebody from Terry's group. Then we had our picture taken with a big cardboard cut-out of Reagan, and I remember thinking it was going to be a very important picture. So, when Terry introduced me on stage, I already felt as if I'd known him for a very long time.' Huge phone bills were duly run up before Armistead invited him out to stay in his cottage on Noe Street for a month to see what happened.

An interesting facet of the relationship which evolved was a Southern background that at once united and divided them. A native of Marietta, Georgia – the home district of Newt Gingrich, Georgia's equivalent of Jesse Helms – Terry cheerfully describes his background as white trash, where Armistead calls his 'tight assed aristocratic'. 'Someone like Terry was extremely exotic to me when I was growing up. I remember driving to the beach with my parents when I was a pre-teen and seeing these shirtless country boys standing in the shadows next to the tobacco barn and thinking of them probably in the way that Joe Orton used to think of those boys from

Tangiers. And going on camping trips to the country with other boys from my scout troop and seeing these country boys who shot out street signs. They didn't talk like us. They were much more sexually exotic creatures.' In one sense, then, Terry was a fantasy made flesh. Armistead freely admits that it's unlikely the fantasy ran both ways and that Terry used to hang around saying, 'Oh gee, I'd like to get one of those tasty pasty white boys from the country club ...' However they had similar responses to their families. Like Armistead Sr, Terry's father showed a great deal of anger and little tactile affection. In addition, Terry claimed the fifteen year age difference only made Armistead sexier, that he liked the grey entering his moustache. 'We always said we were the same gay age because we came out at the same time. Anita Bryant had forced us both into activism in 1977.'

Atlanta having grown stale for him, Terry moved to San Francisco in March with the intention of finding work and his own apartment. He got a job running the office of the Gay and Lesbian Freedom Day Parade but never moved out of Armistead's place. In that first month, as blissful as it had been, Armistead panicked. Had he acted too hastily and done the wrong thing? But having cold feet was only natural in someone who had waited to forty-one before getting married. And sure enough, it got easier and easier. Undoubtedly this was not only because they were in love, but because Armistead began to realize how well Terry managed him. Years later, discussing the directions the relationship was taking, Terry said, 'I took care of you from the beginning. It's my nature to do that.'

Armistead began work on *Significant Others*, the *Tales* novel he would dedicate so touchingly 'To Terry, who took his time getting here', while Terry continued to work for the Gay Freedom Day organization and later established and managed the San Francisco branch of A Different Light, the gay bookstore chain. Six weeks after moving to San Francisco – and three days after his 26th birthday – Terry returned home and announced, 'Now's your chance to get out of it.' With no particular forebodings, he had taken an HIV test so as to be able responsibly to offer Armistead a clean bill of health. Armistead told him he couldn't get out of it because he was already in love with him.

Back then an HIV positive diagnosis was usually a rapidly executed death sentence. Terrified, convinced he had been offered this complete happiness only to lose it in eighteen months or even six, Armistead began making plans. He steered them into a process of conscious memory gathering. They would do the things they had always wanted to do, like going on a pilgrimage to Lesbos with Armistead's cherished ex Steve Beery, who tested HIV positive soon after Terry did. If time was to be short, then they would live it richly. 'There were so many elements, so many life or death elements involved in my relationship with Terry that it just intensified it. To be fighting the beast together just made it all the more powerful.'

As well as working within the San Francisco gay community Terry swiftly became an integral part of Armistead's working life. Scared of nobody, shrewdly assessing the areas where *Tales* could be better produced or marketed, he ran the business that was Maupin with a bulldog tenacity that would make him enemies but dramatically increase Armistead's visibility and earnings. The first evidence of his involvement was the high production values assigned to *Significant Others*, the first of the *Tales* books to be written purely as a novel. Terry decided it should have line drawings for the drop capitals at each chapter heading. He took photographs in the bosky shadows of Bohemian Grove to base them on and helped Armistead select an artist for the job.

By the time I first met them, when they were publicizing *Significant Others*, it was very much 'they' and not 'he' that was being promoted. They rapidly became one of the first self-proclaimed and therefore eagerly mythologized celebrity gay couples. Journalists love a novelty and meeting a gay writer who introduced his lover as part of the package rather than explaining him away as a secretary was just that. Furthermore, Terry was adamant they should be up-front about his HIV status as the publicity would give them an admirable educational platform from which to change attitudes.

This process carried a cost, however. Any couple that promotes itself is at risk of diminishing or smothering the vital relationship behind the ideal image. Terry and Armistead may not have come across as squeaky clean – anyone who met them could see that they were far more interesting, and argumentative, than that – but that was the way the media liked them, at the risk of choking a living thing with treacly sentiment. TV shows were the worst offenders here, hinting at a Desi and Lucy falseness when the pair were actually two very tired, deeply in love people trying not to sound fake. 'It wasn't that it was artificial, after all. We were genuinely in love with each other and genuinely wanting to share it with the world.'

They were photographed waving to British audiences from their bed for Channel Four's notorious *Camp Christmas* and expected to throw open the doors of their lovely new home for the 'Stately Homos' section of *Out on Tuesday*. 'There I was at the tansu saying, "And this is where I keep my dope and this is where Terry keeps his AZT," and I heard my voice starting to sound artificial and strained.'

Whatever the strain on the relationship, their achievement in terms of upping gay visibility in the media was astonishing. 'Terry and I were in the couples section of *People* together – as a couple. And we saw it as a political act to show that two men could be happy together and free to build a life with each other.' But he cites as a warning the example of the Jackson-Parises. Bob Paris, a Mr Universe, came out with his body-builder lover, Rod Jackson. They became a sort of model gay pin-up couple. 'And the whole thing just became too coy and unbearable for some people to handle and they ended up getting attacked. And I think it was very easy for fags to hate them because they were both so cute. And they were nice guys, incidentally.'

By the time they came to England in 1987, Terry was managing Armistead, although even then they were rigorously steering clear of using such a term. Broadway composer John Kander was quite horrified when he heard. 'I told him that Terry was going to take on the role and he said, "This is a big mistake. He'll become your boss." And I laughed at that, you know. I've been in charge of my own life for a long time. It was just nice for once to have someone to make decisions with, whose opinion and taste I could trust. But it does change the dynamics of things a bit. It increases the intimacy and it increases the danger of fights, because you're professionally *and* romantically entwined.'

Terry turned Armistead around, founding an efficient business he called Literary Bent. There were no more bouncing cheques. He organized credit cards, ran the household and business accounts, saw bills were paid on time, organized retirement funds. 'He did all this thinking he would die at any moment.'

The last thing Terry wanted, however, was to become a second Mr Maupin, neither did he seek fame for himself. Armistead did his best, 'But there was always some insensitive asshole out there who would step over him to try to get to me. I would be the lucky one at book signings because people had about half a minute to talk to me and then they had to move on. Terry would get cornered by some bore who would end up asking, you know, "What's it like living with a celebrity?"'

When Terry moved out in May, 1996, Armistead felt pain that easily eclipsed any he had ever experienced. 'I was alternately angry and tearful for a long time. I should have seen it coming, I guess, but I didn't. I thought we were as solid as two people could be. There were a number of reasons for the split, but I think the main one was that Terry needed to be alone, to get in touch with the part of himself that was him and not us. He had already started to make his own friends – people I didn't know – and to have his own adventures, as a way of doing that.'

It should be said that an additional pressure that contributed to the relationship's breakdown was, ironically, Terry's improved health. Like countless couples where one partner is HIV positive, Armistead and Terry had come to build their marriage on the assumption that Terry was going to get sick once too often and die. But brand new options and questions arose when the new drug cocktails and testosterone treatments began to turn Terry from a sickly weakling into a tough guy with muscles to match his attitude, indefinitely suspending his death sentence. 'Learning you're going to live can cause as many upheavals as learning you're going to die. And what happened to us has apparently become commonplace among gay couples. There's even a name for it now: a "cocktail divorce."'

The pair are still inseparable in many ways, still enmeshed through countless ties, not simply those relating to Armistead's work. 'Many of our friends, especially the straight ones, marvel at how we're still such a family. I marvel at it myself. It was amazing to discover that through all the pain and anger our love for each other was a constant. It was like the break-up was the final proof of our permanency. I guess sometimes the heart breaks just so it can get bigger.'

As before, when negotiating with publishers, film producers and booksellers, the two are a formidable double act. 'Terry and I agree with each other, it's just the tactics on which we sometimes differ. I've gone through life being the polite, nice guy who tries way too hard not to offend and as a consequence sometimes gets taken advantage of. And Terry is extremely self-protective and blunt as Hell. But we've been good for each other, I think. He's taught me to take care of myself, and I've taught him to be more tactful.'

The grim truth, of course, is that no experience, however painful, is wasted on a novelist. It's a truism among agents that writers work out their pain through their work and should think twice before carrying it off to a psychotherapist in case the treatment proves successful and eradicates the impulse to write at all. Just as the love of Armistead's life was lived in public, thanks to a decision to promote it on political grounds, so it was being and will continue to be, written out through his narratives.

Daniel

In 1977, the night before the *Chronicle* ran the episode where Brian dares to hold up his phone number for Lady Eleven to read through her binoculars, Armistead picked up Daniel Katz, an ultra cute nineteen-year-old Jewish boy from New York. Most young gay men in the city at that time were on the run from something – tyrannical parents, Catholic seminaries, abusive, closeted relationships. Daniel was a refugee from the Jews For Jesus organization who had treated him traumatically when they found out about his sexuality. He was already a fan of *Tales*.

It so happened that Armistead had been unable to resist the temptation to insert his own phone number as the one Brian holds up ... 'Could not resist seeing what sort of response I would get. And I had lucked out and brought this sweet, gorgeous kid home with me and the phone started ringing. At five o'clock in the morning. Once he realized what was going on, Daniel got into it with a vengeance, answering the phone and hollering down the hall, 'Hey Brian! Get down here. It's another one for you ...'

In the next four years he became, not a significant other but a little brother figure for Armistead, witty, kind, supportive. For a while he lived in a little garden studio across the Filbert Steps from Armistead's place then, in 1979, he moved back to New York to work for the then hot men's clothes designer, Perry Ellis. He died of AIDS on 16 October, 1982. A very early fatality.

> *'He was the person who brought the reality home to me in such a big way that I determined to include it as subject matter in* Babycakes *which, as far as I know, was the first fiction published anywhere to acknowledge AIDS.'* Like Daniel's death, far away in New York, Dr Jon's death happens, as it were, off-stage but is none the less moving for the reader's sudden realization of what has happened since they last saw him in Further Tales.

ARMISTEAD AND STEVE BEERY WITH ARMISTEAD'S VW CONVERTIBLE, 1979

Steve. And Harvey

Some of the sweetest relationships spring up in the sourest of moments. Armistead met Steve at Harvey Milk's memorial service. In the last autumn of Harvey's life, young Steve Beery attended San Francisco's famous Beaux Arts Ball, a masquerade at which society mingles freely with the hoi polloi. Steve had a Batman fixation so was dressed as Robin and the city's first gay supervisor, some twenty years his senior, sidled up and said, 'Hop on my back, Boy Wonder, and I'll fly you to Gotham City.' Steve was already smitten with Harvey from afar so needed no encouragement to become his latest hot young thing. One day that November he was shattered to hear that Supervisor Dan White had burst into City Hall and pumped several rounds into both Mayor George Moscone and Harvey. The shock was made worse when he staggered home, rocked by the news, to find a message from his housemate that Harvey had called that morning proposing a date that night. 'Steve was nearly suicidal. It confirmed the worst he'd ever suspected about mankind, I guess, and I think his mind was sort of fragile at that point anyway.'

Coming to the memorial — held with characteristic panache in the Opera House — was bad enough when Steve knew nobody but was made ten times worse by the discovery that there were already three official Harvey Milk 'widows' and he wasn't one of them. Bewildered, unsupported, he sat, turned to recognize a friendly face and said, 'You're Armistead Maupin aren't you?' He blurted out his story, the way Armistead makes it so easy to do, and they held hands throughout the service.

The latter was a structureless, multi-faith, anti-establishment riot of celebration and shared shock; much what you'd expect from cramming the entire lesbigay and left wing population of San Francisco into an opera house and leaving them to make something up along democratic principles. A lesbian co-worker of Harvey's got up to announce that she'd been trying to decide whether or not it would be more radical to wear black leather or a dress and settled on a dress in Harvey's honour. And so it went on. 'People were crying and laughing all at the same time. It was amazing. It was a second Stonewall.' The difference being that this time the media could not stay away. Armistead also maintains that the premise that the party ended with AIDS had never held water in San Francisco. Milk and Moscone's assassinations had been that city's wake-up call. 'For us *that* was the end of the party. That was the cold confrontation with the reality of people ... *hating*. And it had the same edifying effect as AIDS, with gay family bonds growing even stronger. It was only two weeks away from Jonestown [the mass suicide in Guyana] which was also a San Francisco-based thing. So it was a very surreal time to be living. And it was in a little valley between *More Tales* and *Further Tales* and people always ask, 'Why didn't you mention Harvey Milk?' and I say it was because I wasn't writing.' In fact in the next serial, *Further Tales*, he would have Michael and Brian queerbashed simultaneously to reflect the Milk–Moscone murders.

Two weeks later, Armistead was passing La Contadina on Union Street (where Mrs. Madrigal tells Brian she's transsexual) when he caught sight of an attractive face then saw it was Steve's. 'He was as cute as pie. I described him in the novel [*The Night Listener*] as having the face of a happy rabbit and a sleek, Superhero chest that startled you when the shirt came off. Extraordinary really ... And he came back to my little studio on the Filbert Steps. And that's where the shirt came off and I went, 'Whoa!'

They lived together for a while in the house nestling in what Steve referred to as the pubic hair of Coit Tower. It was a third storey flat with amazing views downtown and across the bay. They painted it a flesh-toned Band-Aid shade described on the tin as Pagoda Pink so inevitably the house was unofficially christened the Pagoda. They were only lovers for a very brief time, but their relationship continued as a romantic friendship in the most life-affirming way. It was Armistead's first taste of eroticized domesticity. They had a shared love of films, of comic strips – Steve was an accomplished amateur cartoonist – and of old movies. Monogamy was regarded as deeply uncool at the time so beyond playing at keeping house, no promises were exchanged. *Playing* was the key word here; every morning before leaving for one of his mindless temp jobs at Kelly Girl, Steve would leave a romantic lyric from a Harry Warren song propped up on the kitchen table. 'I think it was a sort of homage to the thing we'd never really had. And we didn't really have it with each other.'

Arrangements were not on their side however. The flat had only one bedroom and no put-you-up and Steve had a taste for leather that Armistead could not satisfy – a recurrent problem in his life this. 'It became increasingly clear we were cramping each other's style because we were going out to have our adventures and things. You really had to be very careful how you co-ordinated it. We knew that we loved each other as friends but I basically said that we'd have a better chance of finding what we were looking for if we weren't living together.' So Steve moved into the studio across the way just vacated by Daniel Katz moving to New York.

The failed love affair rapidly evolved into giddy friendship so close that for the next seven years they were, to all intents and purposes, each other's significant other. Steve was clever and funny, the perfect travelling or research companion. 'In other ways he was a total kid. He bit his fingernails down to the nub. I know he had a dark side but he never let me see it. He just would go off for a few days and then he'd come back and be sunny again.' Steve went on the cruise to Alaska that Armistead used in *Further Tales*. It was with Steve that Armistead found the Grace Cathedral elevator, and hit on its mysterious keyhole as the perfect solution to the Burke Andrew enigma. 'I remember him standing there in the elevator saying, 'The key. Burke! The key!' We rented a house in the Cotswolds for six weeks in 1986. I'd already met Terry and he'd moved to San Francisco. And Terry sweetly agreed to hold down the fort with Willie the poodle while Steve and I went on this trip on our own.'

In a perfect illustration of the kind of elastic love/friendship bond which straight people have often envied among gay ones, Steve was able to tag along with the new couple on trips and to parties without it causing strain. There was friction occasionally, as in any friendship, but the abiding sense when meeting the three of them together, as when I first met Armistead, was a sort of playground envy; here was a gang that you wanted to join. It was also a relationship that ran right to the heart of *Tales* where Mona, at one point, admits that she'd settle for 'five good friends' and where Michael and Ned, his partner at the nursery, begin as lovers then evolve into more-than-friends. One line, in particular, describes the still loving exes' new arrangement in a way that struck home cruelly for many gay readers, myself included: 'Michael would share his exploits with Ned like a small dog that drags a dead thing home and lays it on the doorstep of someone he loves.'

At the time we are talking, Armistead is struggling to resolve his feelings about Terry taking up with a new lover, Gary Lebow, a man it is impossible not to like. Inevitably he makes comparisons, now that he is in the Steve position, on the outside looking in, wondering if he has Steve's strength of character to make it work. 'What were the elements of that that I loved so much and can I have that with Terry now? It's possible. It really was because it lacked the neurosis of "Is he my one and only?"' But it really was a tremendously comfortable relationship. Because we allowed each other a certain amount of distance and we both knew what our shortcomings were.'

Some of course would argue that it's precisely the comfort and friendliness in a love affair that dooms its passionate content from the start, because with most lovers there's an element of artificial behaviour that keeps the love affair 'sexy'. Honesty, real honesty, leads all too often to sisterhood, which is comforting but rarely sexy. But I digress.

Steve had never really found his métier. Like a lot of gay men he was hugely well informed about a lot of things that would never help land him a job. Bette Midler's discography, for instance. He wrote occasional criticism for *The Advocate* and, when Armistead began writing pieces for *Interview* magazine, came into his own as an informed redactor of the tapes Armistead would make with each subject, skillfully cleaning the transcriptions so that the jokes were funnier and the conversation more polished. It was a dream come true for him meeting the likes of Midler and Warhol but he brought more to the work than that: 'He had this complete, childlike appreciation of these people, coupled with tremendous intelligence and a very analytical mind.'

As well as their closeness in age, one of the reasons Steve and Terry were able to bond so, often to the exclusion of Armistead, was their shared HIV status, having both tested positive in the same year. Steve stayed fairly well, well enough to look after himself, until during the shooting of the first series of *Tales*. Armistead wanted him to join them on a location shoot in his neighbourhood one day – at the Pentshack set based on Armistead's old apartment – and became disturbed when Steve didn't answer the phone. 'Terry and I went over and found him in a stupor, near death, in his sofabed. And he just rolled over and smiled at us, like he'd been snoring or something and we'd shaken him to wake him up. And the ambulance came and took him down the Filbert Steps in a scene that completely recreated what happened to Mouse sixteen years earlier with Guillain-Barré. Very weird. I suppose if you get sick in San Francisco on one of those hills, you'll inevitably be hauled down on a gurney. But Steve was all I could think of when we shot the scene for the miniseries five years later.' The toughest part was persuading Steve to leave the shadow of the Coit Tower to live somewhere more practical for his carers. Eventually Armistead and Terry persuaded him into Maitri, a Zen hospice in the Castro, and were able to take all the pictures off his walls and recreate his room in there.

Shortly before Steve's death in 1993, Armistead and Terry watched Bette Midler shooting the video for her song from *For The Boys, In My Life*. Midler's photographer, Greg Gorman, an old friend of the San Francisco trio, asked The Divine to sign one of his Polaroids for Steve. She wrote, 'Steve, Aloha, Bette,' choosing the Hawaiian greeting because it can mean both hello and goodbye.

'And just two days before he died we came to the hospice with Bette's Art Or Bust *concert video and put it on his machine. He couldn't talk at that point, so we just propped him up in bed with this beatific smile on his face which got bigger when she came out bouncing a huge inflatable boob over her head, and it was basically our memorial service for him before he died. He was aware of it, too – that this was kind of a rite. We all knew the music, and it was more beautiful than*

*it had ever been. Bette sings an anthem at the end, 'Here Comes The Flood',
which was like saying, "He's dying." And Terry and I cried on each other, and
part of the reason we were crying was it felt like a sort of dress rehearsal for his
own death.'*

At Steve's request, his body was cremated and the ashes buried in his front
yard under a new rosebush – another homage to Midler. Also present at
this ceremony were Louise and Darryl Vance, old friends of Terry's from
Atlanta who had moved to San Francisco to be closer to their HIV-positive
friend and had become part of his new family. 'Louise brought some little
stone hearts that we threw into the hole with the ashes, and it was very
low-key and lovely. And I remember being able to distance myself from
my grief. I still haven't gotten it all out, I'm sure. Because I thought, "it'll
be worse the next time because there won't be any arms you can cry in like
you can with Terry."'

Big Armistead and Diana, two

News of Harvey Milk's assassination broke on the last day of a visit from Diana and Armistead Sr. It was an intensely moving visit in any case because they already knew that Diana had inoperable cancer and the chief purpose of the trip was to let her and Armistead spend time together in case the chance never arose again.

Arrangements had already been made for the three to go out to dinner to Armistead's friend Dave Kopay near Twin Peaks. This was a big educational step for them, even though Armistead Sr was no great sports-lover, because Dave was very famous at the time as the only openly gay professional football player. He had played with the Washington Redskins and other teams, had his story made into a book and he was one great lunk of a guy – as far from the 'fairy nice gentleme' of the Raleigh Little Theatre as a loving son could hope to lay on for them. Dinner at Dave's consisted of an assortment of beers and a barrel of Kentucky Fried Chicken on the table – about as jock-like as you could get. 'But my father was seriously confused because Dave took him into his bedroom and showed him Polaroids of women and men that he'd messed around with, so my father came out and said, "What's the matter with that boy? Doesn't he know he's queer?"'

Dinner over, Diana was weak and ready for bed, while Armistead and the rest of the Duck House gang wanted to join the candlelight march that had been hastily announced in the wake of the assassinations. 'So we all piled into David's Toyota pick-up, including my parents scrunched into the back – it was a flatbed basically. And someone passed a joint around and I waited to see what the response was going to be. And my father looked at it for a moment and then he said, "Give me that goddammed thing!" and he took a toke off of it himself, as if to say, "I have to have *something* to help me deal with what's

ARMISTEAD AND HIS MOTHER AT LITTLE CAT FEET, CIRCA 1973

going on here!"' Diana and Armistead Sr were dropped off on Market Street so they could return to their hotel. It was a poignant parting, Armistead wondering how his mother would look when next they met or even if they'd get to meet again at all. These thoughts were still in his mind as they were jostling their way to the stage in front of City Hall when one of his friends spotted Diana and Armistead Sr on the other side of the crowd, on their own, drawn in out of curiosity. Deeply moved, Armistead called them over only to be horrified as Joan Baez took the stage. To Armistead Sr, La Baez was the Wicked Witch of the West but both he and Diana held respectful silence. 'The whole experience was too overwhelming to comment on. It was just a sea of candlelight. It looked like lava moving across the city. We felt community and love more than anything else. Lots of people, including me, were consumed with rage, but it wasn't being shown that night.'

Armistead felt in this moment that his whole life had come together at last. His parents had met his extended family and seen they were all intelligent, presentable guys. Furthermore he was able to show them he had become something of a celebrity for being himself and feel their respect for that.

The timing of the visit was well judged in more ways than one. Diana died the following year. Armistead had spent four months living in Los Angeles at the Chateau Marmont with a view to researching an LA version of *Tales* for the *Los Angeles Herald Examiner* but failing to get a satisfactory hold on the project. He was still there when a call came through from his sister in Raleigh. 'Jane had been caring for my mother, and she told me very gently that it was time to come home.'

He and his father camped out in the hospital room like gypsies the day Diana died, refusing to be chased off by the nurses at the end of visiting hours. While she was sleeping, Armistead Sr admitted he was sorry he had not brought up the subject of Armistead's gayness earlier because it would have made the pain a bit less for his son. 'Looking back this seems so uncharacteristic of him. Whether he was softened by his grief or my mother had actually told him to talk to me I don't know. But I was touched. And my mother seemed to be in the driver's seat for the first time in her life. She was giving orders right and left. She told me which relatives would not be allowed in the room; she'd tolerated them all her life and she didn't have to anymore. She told me that I should write a "sweet" book one day I don't think she quite understood – *Tales* was still too nasty for her. And she told me to come back in the morning because she had an orderly she wanted me to meet. She was trying to fix me up! It was an amazing time.'

'GRANNIE' MARGUERITE SMITH BARTON IN COSTUME AS THE MADWOMAN OF CHAILLOT, EARLY FIFTIES

The first Mrs Madrigal?

Armistead constantly fights the pressure on him to name the originals of the characters in *Tales* and there are certainly no tidy parallels between his address book and the cast list. However even he acknowledges that the principal inspiration for Mrs Madrigal – the generous free spirit, not the transsexual – was the magnificent maternal grandmother he called Grannie.

An ardent suffragist and popular public speaker in Britain, Marguerite Smith Barton married an old school Victorian patriarch thirty years her senior. Or rather she *appeared* to have married him. Years later we were to discover through a mutual friend and Chatto and Windus contact, Kate Hardy, that Armistead and she were related through his grandfather, but that the relationship was on the wrong side of the sheets because Grandpa had been married to Kate's great-grandmother but never – legally – to Armistead's grandmother. He had left behind a wife and several children when Marguerite became pregnant with Diana, moving with her to America, where as a young man he had helped establish the Bessemer steel process in Alabama. They settled in the mountains of North Carolina in a house they called Pineburr Lodge and raised five further children and even more Great Danes. He then died, leaving her in a still strange country to support this tribe on her own.

Marguerite had been an independent and artistic soul back in Britain. She had studied piano and, in her early teens, had been the youngest girl in England to pass the senior exams of the Royal College of Music. As a young women she gave dramatic recitations and lectures on such subjects as 'Eastern Philosophies,' 'The Symbolism of Colour' and 'Physical Culture for Women,' and began a lifelong interest in Theosophy and palm reading. She was an adept at the latter, to the point where she would at once embarrass and delight her grandchildren by 'eavesdropping' on people's hands and destinies in public, especially in church.

Armistead was entirely in her thrall from an early age. Hardly surprising given that, within the respectable certainties of Raleigh, she held all the potency of a full-blooded camp icon. His first memory of Grannie is her rising in a fog of dry ice from the stage trapdoor of the Raleigh Little Theatre in the title role of Giraudot's *The Madwoman of Chaillot*. He adored her because in a family where a son's every career move was mapped out for him at birth, she allowed him to be himself from the very beginning. 'She was always trying to figure out who I was, not tell me who I should become.' He remains convinced that she sensed he was gay even when he was a child. 'She used to talk about her bachelor cousin, Curtis and all their "artistic" friends. And I have a very strong feeling that she had a lot of gay friends, whether she knew it or not ...'

She used to read his palm as a child and would often break off in the midst of her reading to ask what he planned to do with his life. When he spouted the family line about becoming a lawyer and joining Big Armistead's firm she would gently close his palm, pat it and change the subject, discreetly indicating her disbelief but not wanting to cause trouble.

She remained physically and mentally alert into her nineties, when she could still hold her own at cocktail parties 'I used to be so proud of her. I watched her, one time, reading the palm of the governor of North Carolina.'

Destined to outlive Diana, her beloved eldest daughter, by a few months, she was living in a rest home in Alexandria, Virginia in 1978. Armistead paid her a last visit there and was warned by an aunt that she had lost many of her faculties finally and would probably not recognize him. 'It was a sort of high rise where they had residential units and they moved the infirm to a hospital on the top floor. Grannie was still in an apartment, but I was really surprised to see her because she was quite white haired and as long as I could remember, she'd dyed her hair this colour called *champagne beige*. Everything was beige. She had beige hats and beige feathers in them. Beige suits. So her hair had turned white but she still had these bright blue eyes. And she treated me very politely but, as my aunt had predicted, exactly like a stranger. *Tales* had just been published as a book and

I tried to brag about it but she didn't get who I was or what the book was or anything. So I was just about ready to leave when I had one last brainstorm and thrust my hand out in front of her. And she took my hand and sat there reading my palm as if it were a book, to herself. And finally she said, "Teddy! You're in your thirties now!"'

She told him she could see from his palm that he had made the right decisions creatively, admitted that she had known when he was eight or nine that he would never be a lawyer. 'Then she made a little sort of airy-fairy speech to me about how she would be the breeze in the room I felt sometimes, to let me know that I wasn't alone ... She was very important to me. And Anna, the whole idea of Anna Madrigal, was based on her spirit.'

All these years later, we are walking along Sunset Boulevard on our way to a movie when we pass a palm reader. I sense Armistead is feeling sore still, both from the outcome of the Emmys and the upheavals in his love life so when he notices the sign as well I grab the chance of a diversion and urge him in. The urban gypsy who greets us is a far cry from Grannie. A hard bitten creature, with a face of stone, she announces her price is per palm. When, automatically, Armistead holds out both, she charges him double. Her routine is clumsy, spiked with a constant 'Am I right?' refrain as she probes for clues. 'I see pain. You've been in a lot of pain but you're getting through it now, am I right? You have success. Lots and lots of success but the money means less to you than the heart, am I right? Things haven't been easy for you. I see tears. I see change.'

Suddenly, maddeningly, I am banished onto the street, ostensibly so my thoughts won't 'interfere with the reading' but actually so she can turn a hard sales pitch for several in-depth therapeutic sessions onto the man whose pain would have been evident to a child the moment we came in. As we move on towards a nasty film about heartless people and their vicious love lives, we try to laugh off our folly and make each other giggle by imitating her tacky patter but the encounter leaves an unpleasant edge on the evening that lingers for hours like a bad smell.

Further Tales

Further Tales of the City, the third year of the *Chronicle* serial becomes noticeably more autobiographical than its predecessors. The Rock Hudson experience is in there as Michael's fling with Blank Blank. The relationship with Steve Beery, romance-turned-buddydom, is in there as Michael's friendship with Ned the gardener. Crucially it's also at this point that we see Armistead's growing awareness that he was living in a community that at once 'comforted and oppressed' him, typified when Michael says to Ned, 'Hot Jocks. Hot Cops. Hot This. Hot That. Fourteen shades of jockstraps. There's gotta be a better way to be gay!' and Ned replies, 'You could be a lesbian ...'

> *'The interesting thing about Ned and Michael was that in some ways it was me and Steve. I was the older man. I was ten years older than Steve. In some ways I was Ned and in some ways I was Michael. And they were the two sides of me that were constantly warring; the guy who's completely comfortably in his sexuality and part of this so-called gay community and another side that says, "This is beginning to feel sort of heartless and mechanical." So I just allowed those struggles to go on within those conversations.'*

The adventure story involving DeDe and her twins was heavily influenced by Steve's love of comic books, in particular the fond memories he and Armistead shared of Disney's Huey, Dewey and Louie adventures, 'when they would all go off to some exotic part of the world and fly around in biplanes.' Moments of local colour – like the gay rodeo and the arrival home of the Gay Chorus – now drew on Armistead's experiences as a gay celebrity; in real life he had been master of ceremonies at both events.

Just as *Further Tales* showed Mary Ann Singleton beginning to get slightly drunk on her first few sips of media stardom, so Armistead could no longer pretend that he was merely writing a short-lived column for a provincial newspaper. He had already been offered a teasing taste, at least, of how it might feel to write for posterity. At the end of the second year, when the sequence later known as *More Tales* was finished, an editor in New York, Harvey Ginsberg, had contacted him to say he'd read several episodes while staying on the West Coast and thought there might be a book in it.

Tales and *More Tales* were tweaked and edited and published as novels. They were not an instant success, partly because Harper and Row (part of the company now known as HarperCollins) were uncertain how to publish them. *Tales* was among the first of the new wave of trade paperbacks in America and was correspondingly under-reviewed. Both it and *More Tales* came out as oversized pamphlets, in paperback, with light, cartoony covers, in the first instance merely a map, which gave no explanation of the contents, nothing even to indicate that it was a novel. 'It was almost as if they were too embarrassed to tell you what was actually inside. Or maybe because they thought it would sell in San Francisco and nowhere else and that San Franciscans would know what it was.'

Tales as a novel was initially a failure with large numbers of returns. Armistead took its future into his own hands, Jeffrey Archer style, and began to call on bookstores. In particular, he singled out the freshly sprung-up gay bookshops – who at that stage were grateful for appearances by *any* authors, however unknown – and began to sell the books on the back of his wittiness as a reader and performer. It was this process that contributed so much to his becoming thought of as a gay author rather than one who wrote about gay subjects among other things. 'The irony was that I had to convince them that there was a gay market when we first started selling the book. I said, "Put something on the jacket that indicates there's something in here for gay people." And they were very wary of doing that. I remember my editor saying to me, "Oh Armistead. *Toujours* gay. *Toujours* gay." Then in later years, when I'd really got my foothold, they were trying to angle it exclusively to the gay market. When I was trying to say to them, "Look, there's nothing about this story that won't appeal to the *general* population. Stop confining me to this area," they didn't understand. Back at the newspaper I had already felt the exhilaration of being a big old queer in a mainstream context. Nothing was more fun. It struck a blow for freedom and let you be part of the world at the same time. And I knew I could do that on a national scale. In those days I didn't *dream* of an international scale. But I felt it would work eventually for the rest of America and they finally had the sense to sell it that way.' However, back when he was still at work on the third series, he was trying to think of himself as a novelist – despite still being paid a reporter's salary – but everything was militating against it.

ARMISTEAD, TERRY AND WILLIE, AT 655 1/2 NOE STREET. PHOTOGRAPHED
FOR THE ADVOCATE IN 1986

Serial serial killer

There are several elements in *Tales* the newspaper serial that never appeared in *Tales* the novel sequence. Armistead jumped at the chance to make changes in repackaging the serial in book form. Writing it on a day-to-day basis, quite without the leisure to plot and construct the way a novelist might, he had left unsightly creases he now wanted ironed out. Not the least of which was allowing Mary Ann and Michael to sleep together at the end of the first serial. Even today he winces at the thought of having once allowed these two cherished characters to be each other's Yuletide mercy fuck.

More bizarre still, to cognoscenti unfamiliar with the original, will be the little business of a serial killer stalking through the first year's episodes. As a central plot string, which he claims he inserted because he was convinced readers would not be sufficiently held by his characters' love lives or lack of them, he created the Tinkerbell Killer. Loosely based on the real life Zodiac, this maniac strangled women with pantyhose and sprinkled them with blue glitter. The link with Mary Ann's life was two-fold because Halcyon Communications handled the Adorable Pantyhose account and her old friend and Pet Rock lover, Connie Bradshaw, ended up as one of the Tinkerbell Killer's victims. Doubt was cast on all of the characters, even Mrs Madrigal. A bumbling cop called Inspector Tandy was on the killer's trail. His best friend at the station was a real-life San Francisco policeman, Dave Toschi, who Armistead interviewed, drawing on his experiences hunting the elusive Zodiac, to inject some verisimilitude into the tale.

Armistead began to receive fan letters specifically praising Dave Toschi, asking that he be retained in the column. There were even some signed by all the girls in a dorm. He thought nothing of it at the time and set them on one side. Then two years later, in the summer of 1978, just two months before

Tales of the City was due to be published in book form, the Zodiac sent another letter to the *Chronicle*. It was his first since the Sixties, when he had last struck. Apparently he or she had started to miss the publicity. As before, the paper ran the letter on its front page. Armistead's blood froze as he read it. 'The whole language of the letter was B movie, tough guy dialogue. It sounded fake. And it said, "That city pig Toschi is tough, but I'm tougher."' The serial killer was taunting the man who was chasing him, and *plugging* him as well. And I had this really creepy suspicion.' Digging through his old fan-mail he found the letters praising the Toschi character and only now realized they'd all been typed on the same typewriter and that they matched the typing in a couple of letters Toschi had sent Armistead. It was a distinctly *Jagged Edge* moment.

Armistead and fellow Duck Houser, Ken Maley took the letters to the police station and asked for a confidential audience with the Chief of Intelligence. 'I expected to be told I'd gone completely off the deep end, but the guy just shook his head and said, "this sure sounds like him all right". Clutching this A1 journalistic scoop, Armistead went to *New West* magazine (the one where Burke Andrew publishes his cannibal exposé ...), told them what he had and called a press conference. Every reporter in the city came. Rumours had spread so furiously it was thought that Armistead had evidence that Toschi actually was the Zodiac killer – simply because in *Tales* the bumbling cop was exposed as the Tinkerbell Killer – and few stories sell more papers than fresh developments in an unsolved murder mystery. When this turned out not to be the case and when, furthermore, Armistead refused to give full details until his *New West* piece appeared, the reporters savaged him.

'I can remember one particular reporter, a woman from a local TV station that I still can't stand, saying, "You're no writer. What makes you think you're a writer?" The idea was that the fluffy fag who wrote this silly little serial had shown the nerve to step into the realm of hardcore journalism and point out something that they had been avoiding for years. Because it was much more glamorous to promote the story of the hardworking cop chasing the killer. And then they really turned on me because the cops, in an effort to cover their own asses, removed Toschi from the Zodiac squad and put him on the pawn shop

detail. And my own newspaper, the Chronicle, *sent a reporter over to his house to write a long, weepy story about this poor, decent, Catholic man with a wife and children, who'd been destroyed by this pulp writer.'*

It was the worst time of Armistead's life so far, matched only by three traumas since. Every self-doubt he had about himself surfaced. He felt the entire town hated him and seriously considered moving to London. It was little comfort when the police subsequently – but privately – admitted that the 1978 Zodiac letter was 'probably' from Toschi. In David Hunt's 1997 best-selling San Francisco thriller *The Magician's Tale*, a subplot reproduces most of these events, with a reporter taking Armistead's role. Pure coincidence, of course ...

ARMISTEAD BY DON BACHARDY, 1979, INK ON PAPER

Interview magazine

Around the time when *Further Tales* began to appear in the *Chronicle*, Armistead was approached to become a West Coast correspondent for Andy Warhol's gossipy glossy, *Interview*. He began as one of the celebrities in it. Bob Colacello, its managing editor, came to interview him then offered him the job. It was a dream come true, not only because Armistead got to chat with such sacred monsters as Bette Midler, Joan Rivers and Dyan Cannon and to party at the Playboy Mansion, but because the magazine was a cult and the exposure, however elliptical, would help to build his international profile in a way that his publishers were still failing to do. 'And I had a wonderful time. Scarcely any of those pieces ever appeared without letting the reader know that I was a gay man interviewing them, so it had a political zing to it ... My whole aim was to be casual about it but not avoid it. *Interview* for all it's homo hipness, never did that. Their write-ups about Studio 54 would tell you that "Barry Diller was there with Diane von Furstenberg..." In New York in the late Seventies, when San Francisco was breaking wide open, the closet was very much intact. And it was considered very uncool to talk about being gay.'

Armistead had a close-up view of the New York way of doing things and not acknowledging them – in 1978. As editor of *Esquire*, Clay Felker had commissioned the non-fiction pieces which gave rise to those notorious plunderings of gay culture for straight filmgoers, *Saturday Night Fever* and *Urban Cowboy*. 'It was no accident that both of them starred John Travolta.' Having enjoyed *Tales*, Felker brought Armistead to New York for a fortnight – at the height of the Anvil era – in the hope that he might generate other stories that could prove similarly profitable. Felker had him steered around town by gossip columnist, Liz Smith. 'And I was so naïve that I didn't realize that this nice woman who had discovered the Temple of Aphrodite in Greece, who we kept bumping into, was actually her lover, Iris Love.' Liz took him to Studio 54 to hang out with Bianca Jagger, Halston and co., but even though he got to dance with Robert Latourneaux, the cowboy hustler in *The Boys in the Band*, Armistead was struck by how unliberated the scene was. 'No matter what you hear now, Studio 54 was *not* the coolest place on the planet. What shocked me about New York in those days was the degree to which homosexuality was still a dirty secret. They dealt with it by pretending that they were too sophisticated to discuss it, by acting like they were well beyond it. Well they *weren't* well beyond it because a lot of them were taking beards to public places. There was a handful of dedicated gay activists, like Vito Russo, who were out there making a noise in the streets but it hadn't sifted into the power structure at all. And still hasn't. To the degree that people like Calvin Klein aren't called on their bullshit ... I got a very cold-blooded glimpse of how things work in the seat of communications. That's what New York is, basically. And I began to realize how long I would be marginalized because of my insistence on being honest.'

He was similarly startled when Andy Warhol came on a rare visit to San Francisco and, in between autographing women's breasts at a book signing on Polk Street, wanted only to talk about the local female socialites. It was less that he was closeted, than that he pretended to know nothing. 'He made me draw him a little diagram to show him how the Glory Holes worked and I didn't believe him. You know? I couldn't imagine that he wouldn't know what I was talking about and I felt he was just getting me to perform for him in some way.'

In the early eighties, Armistead was called upon to interview Shirley Temple, a.k.a. Ambassador Black (if you know what's good for you). Sitting in her house in Woodside, she reminisced about her time as ambassador to Ghana. 'We had geckos in our residence,' she enthused. 'I love geckos.' And Armistead said, 'Oh yes. We had geckos in Vietnam. They were wonderful. I had them on the walls of my hooch and they were such friendly little creatures. And we also had something called a Fuck You Lizard.'

It just came out. As Shirley drew back in consternation Armistead frantically backtracked, digging himself into an even deeper hole. 'I know how rude it sounds but they were called that because they actually had a call which sounded very much like that. And when I was a naval officer in Vietnam and we were doing our morning briefing, it used to crack the room up because this very stiff army colonel would be up there with his pointer, describing the operations along the canal, and suddenly you'd hear this little voice that went *fuck you fuck you.*'

Shirley did not crack a smile. Shirley said nothing. Ever the professional, ever the diplomat, she knew the goddamned tape recorder was still running. Armistead duly collected himself and the interview proceeded rather less cozily than before. At the very end, however, once the tape recorder was switched off, Shirley paused in the middle of lighting a cigarette to remark with devastating coolness, 'You know, when I was a little girl, and there was profanity on the set, they would close down the set and there would be no more shooting that day.'

Many years later Armistead and Terry were at the private view of a French Impressionist show at the de Young Museum. They had wandered away from the cocktail party to take in the art and soon found themselves alone in a room full of Caillebottes, including the extraordinarily sexy topless males in *The Floor Scraper.* Or almost alone, for there was The Ambassadrix taking in the musculature. 'Ooh look at *that!*' she breathed. 'Isn't that *extraordinary!*' and without thinking, lulled into a delusion of sisterhood, Armistead came right out with, 'You like that, do you, Shirl?'

Of cat pee and Betty Windsor

When Armistead processed out of the Navy and was briefly adrift in San Francisco before returning to Charleston, he fell in with Jay Hanan, an old friend from Chapel Hill, whose wife, Peggy Knickerbocker, found a tuxedo for Armistead and took him to a fancy party out at Seacliff. 'The fog horns were tooting – as well as a few of the wedding guests – and a straight guy hugged me just for having survived Vietnam. I couldn't believe such a town existed. I felt exactly the way Lieutenant Bardill feels in *Babycakes*.' Jay Hanan, it transpires, had a fun-loving, redheaded sister who called everyone she liked, *Babycakes*. So now you know ...

Babycakes was the last section of *Tales* to be written for the *Chronicle*. (*Significant Others*, written as a novel was serialized in the rival *Examiner*, and *Sure of You* was not serialized at all.) Armistead broke with the *Tales* titles at this point because he wanted to lessen the work's newspaper associations and help the public think of him as a novelist. 'And I'd done enough. I had to do three to get people to keep reading and to understand. Then they got the idea. The whole thing has been a struggle against one conception or another about what I am. A gay writer. Not a gay writer. A novelist. A columnist ...' *Babycakes'* chance inspiration was an apartment swap Armistead agreed to in 1983. Through a mutual friend, he met Oxford don, Philip Lloyd-Bostock, who hungered for a gay old time in San Francisco.

Lloyd-Bostock's flat in Notting Hill was not at all what Armistead was expecting. Its bad stippling and lingering cat pee odour are described in painful detail in *Babycakes*. (A morsel of gay trivia is that the flat was less cruelly immortalized in Adam Mars-Jones' story *The Executor*, in which the buddying hero visits after Lloyd-Bostock's death from AIDS to remove such items as might offend the sensibilities of his sheltered parents ...)

Armistead was miserable. This was his first visit to England since he was twenty-one and he had dire jet lag, constipation and that feline whiff to contend with. He was rescued by Somerset Maugham's grandson, Julian Hope, who lent him his place in Kensington. What Lloyd-Bostock *did* do for Armistead was lend him his colourful friends, the travel writer Lucretia Stewart and Lord Jamie Neidpath, *Babycakes'* dedicatee, whose ancestral pile, Stanway House, provided one of the novel's vivid settings.

The main reason for spending a couple of months in England was to see what could be done to rescue the British editions of *Tales*. The first volume had been luridly published by Corgi and sunk without trace. Patrick Janson-Smith, the editor who had acquired the property, had briefly moved to another list and had been mortified by how ill-advisedly *Tales* had been marketed. He decided to repackage the existing volumes and continue printing the series. 'Patrick stuck with me for years when the books were doing nothing. I would ask him how the sales were going and he would say, "Oh fine, just lovely really, just fine" to keep from depressing me with figures.' One of Armistead's earliest British fans was the painter, Howard Hodgkin, who brought the books to the attention of Carmen Callil at Chatto and Windus. It was there, under the editorship of Christine Carswell that Armistead had his first hardcover publication anywhere with *Significant Others*. Janson-Smith, meanwhile, moved the paperbacks to Transworld's more literary imprint, Black Swan, and Chatto eventually reissued the entire series in hardback omnibus editions.

British readers came to the series with no preconceptions. We didn't care if it had appeared in a newspaper first and East coast or West coast were equally American to us. In the gloom of the Thatcher era, the books brought a touch of subversive warmth and were the cause of many a San Franciscan holiday and not a few optimistic emigrations.

Babycakes begins, in an ironic echo of the first line of *Tales*, with the Queen (Betty Windsor) seeing San Francisco for the first time. The material for this came via Steve Beery. Before leaving *Interview*, Armistead had wangled him a job as the San Franciscan gossip columnist. It was not a success – for all his wit, Steve didn't *know* the people he was expected to chatter about – but he did get to cover the Queen's visit and fed the details back to Armistead. Such as that Charlotte Maillard, the socialite chief of protocol in the city, served Cheerios to the gathered press, 'Because we're going to say Cheerio to the Queen.'

So long, Barbary Lane

Significant Others and *Sure of You*, which rounded the *Tales* series off can be read almost as complimentary volumes. They reveal Armistead's love/hate relationship with gay culture and the wider Californian scene even more than his earlier use of the Ned/Michael dialogues. Shot through with the headiness of new love, *Significant Others* is profoundly romantic in a late Shakespearean sense, playing on coincidences and the enchantment of the woodland that provides much of its setting. *Sure of You* by contrast, is angry and tragic, very much a novel of late Eighties disenchantment. By the end, Mary Ann, once an adorably innocent heroine and as much Armistead's alter ego as her erstwhile bosom buddy 'Mouse', has become a self-serving, unprincipled monster and the certainty of Michael's death casts an unrelieved shadow.

Armistead is adamant that in *Significant Others*, he and Terry are most closely present as the glamorous lesbian parents, DeDe and D'orothea. However, there is much of Terry in Michael's indignant lover, Thack. Terry's HIV status is transferred to Michael for the greater poignancy that brings but the pairing of appeaser/aggressor is richly redolent of the Anderson-Maupin household ...

He instinctively shies away from any too close identification of a real person with one of his characters. Which writer wouldn't? We all want our books to be independent, to stand away from the personal mess of our lives. He will, however, admit that there's a lot of *him* in both Mary Ann and later in Cadence Roth, the dwarf heroine of *Maybe The Moon*. 'There's a lot about ambition in all of my work. A lot about vanity. A lot about fear of abandonment.'

When I interviewed Armistead on the publication of *Sure of You*, he was heartily glad to be shot of *Tales* and eager to write something completely new. The time was right to end it. One more book and it would have beggared belief that all these characters were still in touch with one another. He wanted to leave it pure, not see it peter out and deteriorate like some second-rate TV show that no one has the courage to kill off. But he has never escaped the serial and probably never will. There is a website (www.talesofthecity.com) with a bulletin board called The Barbaryphile Forum which is filled with the chatter of its distinctly obsessive fans, eager to trace Mona's whereabouts or discuss whether he did indeed kill Connie twice.

Far from being disturbed by all this, by the refusal of the books to lie down peacefully and gather some respectable dust, he is delighted. 'I've always had a very strong sense of wanting the readers to relate to the people and places of the stories in a very personal and strong visual way. The way I felt when I was fifteen years old and we drove to Atlanta for the first time and I would look across to some forest with the sun setting through it and wonder if Tara might be in that direction. And I knew that that was a work of fiction. I was not an idiot. But I thought, "But where would it be if it *were* here? This is the very ground they'd have walked on if they *had* existed." I've always wanted to create that sensation. And in the early days of writing, when I was very insecure about what I was doing, what my credentials were and whether or not I was a 'real writer' and whether or not Ed White would sneeze at me, I at least knew that's what I wanted to achieve in the end.'

The musical

In 1990 Armistead made his first return to theatre writing since *La Périchole*. He was approached to write the San Franciscan section of a portmanteau musical called *Heart's Desire* with songs by Glen Roven. The idea was four different American authors writing about love in four different American cities.

Called *Suddenly Home*, Armistead's section drew on the story of a visit his sister paid him when he and Terry were still newlyweds and she was seeking their blessing to marry a man they had already nicknamed 'The Shithead'. 'Looking back on it now it seems a little self-satisfied on my part as I thought "We homos have shown the way as to how to have a happy marriage," when in fact we were just like any other couple. But it was still a righting of the balance, and it was true at the time.'

The piece was also shot through with affectionate memories of the earlier visits Jane had made, when she and Armistead would cruise guys together. 'I remember being at a party with her very early on. After she knew that I was gay we really enjoyed that closeness. And there was a really cute guy across the room that she had her eyes on and I, in my smug way, was saying, "Oh forget it. He's *mine*! You know he's completely gay." And she proved me completely wrong and ended up going home to Marin with him.' Although the similarities with Mary Ann and Burke petered out the next day when Jane found herself bumping down a mountain with him fearing for her life while he was down on the floor snorting some precious powder he'd spilled.

The musical had a curious genesis. First Armistead wrote it as a short story for Glen Roven's approval. Then it had to be turned into dialogue scenes, then Glen Roven worked over it putting in the songs, then it was polished to make the dialogue work better. 'And when it was all done, I went back and took what I'd learned from the process of the musical and rewrote the story.' Thus the story, *Suddenly Home*, published in the Faber Book of Gay Short Fiction (edited by Ed White) began as a short story, became a musical and then a short story again. 'So it does have a curious vitality to it because you can really hear the voices speaking to you.'

Heart's Desire was workshopped before finding a home, ironically enough, in the Cleveland Playhouse, the pride of the town Mary Ann had abandoned for San Francisco. It ran for a month, and reviews were mixed, though Armistead's section was universally praised. The show has never since been performed.

Bali Ha'i she calls you

In early 1990, Armistead and Terry were touring Australia and New Zealand to promote *Sure of You*. The last leg of the tour lay around New Zealand's South Island where they then took a week off to explore in anonymity. A friend in Sydney had recommended they stay at the White Rose Lodge in Akaroa, a pretty, 'French-influenced' town on the tip of the Banks Peninsula. The place bowled them over, less the little town, which verges on the twee, than the ravishing natural harbours, rolling hills and white sandy beaches that lie around it. Their landlady saw the light in their eyes and sent them across the bay to Wainui where there was a colonial farmhouse for sale at the top of a dirt track, with wrap-around views. They fell in love with the serene beauty of the place, which Armistead described not only as healing but 'like the ideal of rural America minus the rednecks'. They made an offer and opened a New Zealand bank account on the spot needing only a glimpse of the tiny Hector's dolphins that breed in Akaroa Harbour to make up their minds. That summer, when it was winter in New Zealand, Terry returned alone to supervise the renovation of Kahikatea. When the couple saw the finished product for the first time, the bedroom boasted a huge sunken bath in its bay window and the verandah floorboards were safe enough to dance on. 'It was such a joyous moment, to see this magic hideaway he'd created for the two of us.'

The next five months were the happiest time of Armistead's life. 'I was deep deep deep in love with Terry. I felt so safe there because we'd built this little world for ourselves away from everything. I just woke up in the morning happy, because for one thing there was this ridiculous chorus of birds. And it's ironic because we should have had the greatest fear at that point for Terry's health, which in a way I did. But it was almost as if we had kept it at bay somehow, as if AIDS wouldn't be able to find its way to the place.' They spent happy hours foraging for antiques and old books in Christchurch, stocking the house. Terry has the sort of personality which hates the short days of winter, finding they plunge him into a deep depression, so the idea initially was to live in perpetual summer and spring, swinging between San Francisco and this rural idyll.

They loved escaping the very self-reflexive world of gay California but they sensed it could not last for ever. Periodic reminders came in the shape of Terry's T-cell test results. 'I used to try to play out the scenario in my head of what was I going to do when Terry died. And I knew I wouldn't want to be there by myself. I would try to imagine going into Christchurch to some pathetic little gay bar before dragging some poor creature back to this cottage in the woods and boring him silly with talk about Terry.'

It fulfilled many of Armistead's dreams, however, not least the ones seeded by biographies of Maugham and Coward – 'these photographs you'd always see of five or six friends sitting in lawn chairs at Goldenhurst during a long summer evening.' If you believe your lover is dying, there's a sense in which quality of shared time becomes more important than length and Kahikatea rendered up quality time to the nth degree. It was also a marvellous place in which to write. Despite the cliché of the author scribbling on scraps of paper in the corner of a crowded bistro, most novelists require a measure of comfortable dullness in their lives so that their narrative in progress can effortlessly become the most compelling thing in the day before them. The isolation and picturesque tedium, which admittedly drove Terry half wild with frustration at times, were the perfect pool on which to float a new novel.

The book in question, *Maybe the Moon*, grew at a cracking pace for several reasons. For one thing, the woman who had inspired it died suddenly back in Los Angeles, saddening Armistead but throwing the heroism of her life into sharp relief and freeing him to write her story without the inhibitions that had so-far plagued him. 'She knew I was writing it, and she was thrilled, but I fretted constantly about messing with her life. I remember telling her to think of the character not as herself but as her little sister.'

And there was something else that focused Armistead's attention. Years before, the trip to Lesbos with Terry and Steve had been enlivened by Armistead's wheeze of mailing a packet of pot to await him in the poste restante on the island, cunningly addressed to Anna Madrigal from a Mona Ramsey at 28 Barbary Lane. Armistead was appalled on arriving in the Lesbian post office to find that the poorly wrapped drug was stinking the place out. No one seemed to have noticed, however, or to care and he was able to collect it unchallenged. For his first Christmas at Kahikatea, he received more dope from a friend, loosely packed with a Christmas ornament. Lent courage by two such successful smugglings, he went on, just before he returned in 1991, to try it again. So there they were, in their nightshirts enjoying breakfast with a guest from America one morning, when two cars pulled into the driveway, full of people. Armistead assumed they had missed the turning for the campsite at the bottom of the hill until they identified themselves as New Zealand federal agents.

While sniffer dogs checked out every room and specialists took fingerprints, the senior agent showed Armistead a series of photographs of the offending parcel and asked if it looked familiar. 'Does the name Anna Madrigal mean anything to you?' he asked. 'And my first thought was, 'Yes and if you were literate it would mean something to *you!*' Armistead bit his tongue, however, and fell back on his planned defence of blaming some well-meaning but misguided fan led astray by the quantities of dope smoked throughout *Tales* and distributed by the parcel's fictitious addressee to her lodgers.

'It's all very funny now but it was one of the most panicky moments of my life. It was right up there with the Zodiac thing and Rock Hudson. It was a terrifying thing. I remember they even took a handwriting analysis... They left and we drove into Christchurch together. And we talked all the way as if they might be listening because we thought they could have put a bug on the car. We were completely *paranoid. I can't remember ever having drink because my nerves needed calming but I downed four sherries in a local restaurant in an effort to ease the pain of it. It was really really scary because I felt I had fucked up the idyll by doing this careless thing. The house could have been taken away from us. And then I could go to jail or be asked to leave the country. I suppose they thought that when they searched*

KAHIKATEA, WAINUI, NEW ZEALAND, 1991

the house that they were going to find some huge operation and they didn't. It's kind of silly if you really analyse it because people all over New Zealand grow very good pot ...'

What undoubtedly saved them was a woman federal agent coming back in triumphantly clutching what she thought was a serious drug only to hear that it was Terry's AZT. Plainly sensitivity took over and it was decided that the best punishment was simply not to tell Armistead what action, if any, was going to be taken. He waited for two months until he was sure it was all over, terrorized at regular intervals because the Gentle Annie washing machine sounded like a police siren when it hit the spin cycle. In addition he was now fretting constantly about Terry's health, so writing became his only escape from his nerves. 'If I sat idle for a moment, my mind went crazy. And writing provided the discipline and the focus that I needed to get my mind off other things. But I wrote several of Cady's bleaker moments when I was feeling that way myself ... Experience had stretched me so bare I couldn't keep up the usual cheerful exterior. It was very creepy.'

It was a complete surprise to learn that he had this bedrock of fear in his normally placid soul. He wrote a long letter to Ian McKellen in an effort to work it out of his system. 'And I remember writing "Why are we filling these bookshelves with hundreds of books when he's going to be dead in a year?"'

After spending three San Franciscan winters in sunny Wainui, Terry began to kick against the routine they had mapped out for themselves and, after a few rows about changed minds, it was decided to sell the place. Wonderful though the experience had been, their life there had come to consist chiefly of 'cheese eating and TV watching,' which was doing nothing for Armistead's figure and little for their relationship. 'Fundamentally you don't change because you go to another place. You're still doing whatever it is you do at home. I gained a great deal of weight there. By the time we were touring for *Maybe The Moon* I was really fat. I gave in to the sheer indolence and domesticity, the comfort of it, the ease of having one other person in my life. And a lot of roomy nightshirts!'

Happily, Armistead's sister and her second husband, Joe Yates – who, Armistead hastens to add, was not 'The Shithead' – were looking for somewhere to retreat to and were in a position to buy it. They have since expanded the house as a bed-and-breakfast and raise llamas on the property.

TAMMY AND ARMISTEAD AT THE DUCK HOUSE (1979) BEFORE SHE WAS E.T.
NOTE THE SERIOUS DISCO DUDS

Ladies and gentlemen, Miss Cadence Roth

By way of making a clean break from the *Tales* universe, for his first non-Barbary Lane novel Armistead concentrated on Los Angeles. In part the narrative grew out of a genuine affection for the down-at-heel side to the city he had developed during his period of researching the LA version of *Tales* that never was. In greater measure, however, it was a tribute to an extraordinary friend who happened to be thirty-one inches tall.

He met Tammy, full name Tamara De Treaux, in 1979 on a cruise on San Francisco bay. A local TV show had invited all its guests of the year so Armistead went with his footballer friend, Dave Kopay. 'And I stepped on Tammy. We were making our way to the bar, people were waiting in line to get drinks, and I backed up and heard this voice say, "Watch it, Buster!" And I looked down and there was this miniature Bette Midler. Curly red hair, little short fat arms, virtually no legs, big torso, wonderful funny, laughing face. And a naked fag hag.'

Before becoming an actress and hitting Hollywood in a succession of roles in which she was usually masked in latex or fur, Tammy had found great solace in the gay bars of the East Bay where she had grown up with her mother, soon discovering that these were places where no one would stare. At least, not until someone hoisted her onto a stool and she could hold forth to an audience. She was a shameless flirt and within ten minutes of Armistead's treading on her, had wheedled her way onto Dave Kopay's lap, which Armistead would not have minded doing himself, and was casting glances as if to say, 'Wouldn't you like to sit here? Hmm? On *that?*'

'I had a number of feelings about her. The first was an enormous sense of self-consciousness because she was so extremely different, and I was extremely concerned

about not hurting her feelings and doing the right thing and being the good little boy around her. And yet, like most people who are comfortable with themselves, whether they're black or gay or whatever, Tammy always turned it on herself. I called her up one time when I saw her making a thirty second appearance in the movie, Earth Girls are Easy. *Somebody opened a refrigerator door and she's supposed to be a gremlin in the refrigerator, waggling her fingers in her ears. So I called up and said, "I've seen your latest* tour de force," *and she said, "Oh, you mean* The Midge in the Fridge ..."

From the day they met, Tammy began pestering Armistead to write her extraordinary story and, although this would take over ten years, she made a fleeting first appearance in his work in *Babycakes*. She had been asking him to write a character she could play when *Tales* made it to the screen. 'Okay,' he joked, 'you can be the Queen's manicurist.' Enter Miss Treves, dwarf manicurist to Betty Windsor and mother of Simon Bardill, the gay lieutenant who jumps ship from *Britannia* so as to stay in San Francisco. The name, of course, was an extra joke between them, Treves being the surname of the kind doctor in *The Elephant Man*.

Towards the end of her short life, when he finally decided to write her story, or a story inspired by her story, he invited Tammy to come on a visit so that he could get the answers to the awkward, personal questions he had never dared ask. He was shocked at how much she had changed, how much weight she had put on. She now had to walk with a stroller device and was exhausted by any great exertion. The Fair Oaks Street apartment was a fourth floor walk-up. She took one look and swore she could only leave it if they promised to carry her. When they returned that night after a dinner with novelist Firdaus Kanga, they had a hilarious encounter on the stairs with a dipso neighbour who had to look twice at Armistead and Terry's giggling burden to be sure his eyes were not deceiving him.

Armistead recently stumbled on the notebook from that visit and found some details he regrets having left out of the novel, one of which was her fear that when men were interested in her they would prove to be closet pederasts looking for a quick fix. She had a sex life but not nearly as adventurous or romantic as the one her friend bestowed on her fictional counterpart, Cadence Roth. In real life she was forever falling in love with gay men.

Apart from her size, the main element of Tammy's story that entered *Maybe the Moon* was her having been one of the performers to swelter inside a cutesome alien suit in *ET* along with some other little people, including a legless boy who walked on his hands. The producers were desperate to keep their contributions quiet so as not to spoil the 'magic' of Spielberg's blockbuster and were outraged when Tammy took her story to the tabloids, forcing them to allow all the uncredited dwarf performers to give interviews alongside her in *People* magazine. It struck Armistead that here was a perfect metaphor for the way Hollywood continued to use the talent of gay people while concealing their sexuality. Just as the Hollywood closet is full to bursting, so, once you bother to look, its films are stuffed with performances from dwarfs, usually concealed in the credits as puppet operators. Film makers are forced to use dwarfs because they could never get away with treating child actors in the same way and by employing dwarfs they can win brownie points for employing a minority. 'You would have somebody on your case if you were sticking kids into those little penguin suits in *Batman Returns*.'

He never intended the novel to be an attack on Spielberg, although some read it that way. 'He's obviously a decent man with a conscience. He must be, given the subject matter he's tackled over the years.' It was just bad luck that Spielberg had made the film of which Armistead's elf parable, *Mr Woods* is a parody. *Maybe the Moon* is a very angry book, even more so than *Sure of You*, fired by rage not just at Hollywood's double standards but at a sense of a pervasive American hypocrisy rooted in an almost infantile desire to hold the dream whatever the moral cost. 'And *Maybe the Moon* gave me the perfect disguise in which to be angry. I wasn't Armistead Maupin being angry, I was a thirty-one inch Jewish female dwarf and *boy* was I pissed off!'

There was no come-back from Hollywood when the novel was published but then, as Armistead wryly observes, it's not a community noted for a hunger for literature. The response from little people, however, was warmly affirmative, to the point where Armistead and Terry were guests of honour at a Little People of America convention in Denver. 'Not just dwarfs but women who are five feet tall have told me how much it spoke to their experience.' A review in the *New York Times*, however, referred to the lead character as a 'grotesque' who knew far too much about S & M 'for someone who has to be lifted in and out of cars'. 'The subterranean accusation there is that I'm writing about a gay man, which is an accusation that can only be made when the writer is out of the closet. Never mind that I had a friend who was *just* this way and would discuss any number of sexual issues, largely because she *did* hang out with gay men.'

But dwarf sex, indeed inter-racial dwarf sex, is a far cry from the relatively accessible love lives of the *Tales* characters however complicated they got. 'It's surprising. It's a very difficult subject matter for a lot of people, especially straight women. And I think there's an element there of 'there but for the grace of God go I' and their reaction to that is to turn away.' Women's politics in the early nineties was still partly concerned – when was it not? – with reclaiming their right to independent sexual satisfaction and feminist critics were, perhaps understandably, suspicious of any male writer getting in on the act.

So unlike the last volume of the *Tales* series, *Maybe the Moon* had a slow start and did not make the *New York Times* best-seller list, though it did become a number one best-seller in the UK. Ironically, given that it was designed to be an unfilmable novel, interest in making a movie was almost immediate. Foremost in the actresses after the property was Daryl Hannah, who wanted to play Cady's ditzy roomate, Renee. She would show up for meetings in LA having had to dodge the paparazzi because she was dating John Kennedy Jr at the time. (In fact, the actress gave the book to Jacqueline Onassis in hospital, asking her opinion, and received a letter from the former book editor explaining why it would work as a movie. Hannah later told Armistead it was probably the last book Jackie ever read.) Armistead wrote the adaptation himself, which he describes as 'a real learning experience. I was surprised because I thought, "Oh this book is so dialogue driven, it'll be easy." And of course almost none of the original dialogue survived. And then you often see ways to improve it. Now there are things in the screenplay that I wish I'd put in the novel. I wish I'd given her *a* moment on the stage, for instance, before she has her heart attack.' When we last spoke about it in September 1998, the script was still tentatively close to acquiring finance, years after its completion. The sad part, of course, is that Tammy is no longer around to play the lead role that would fit her like a glove. Cady's obituary at the end of the novel is Tammy's word for word with only her and Spielberg's names changed.

ARMISTEAD WITH CHRISTOPHER ISHERWOOD AND DON BACHARDY IN DON'S
STUDIO, EARLY EIGHTIES

Christopher and his kind

There's a story Armistead likes to tell about Sam Stewart. By the time they met, Stewart was an elder statesman of gay San Francisco, in his late Seventies. He had just published a book called *Parisian Lives*, a memoir of his years in the French capital in the thirties when he was pals with Gertrude and Alice et al. He also wrote a series of witty murder mysteries in which Stein and Toklas were the sleuths. He is best known, funnily enough, for the one-handed fiction he churned out under the *nom de guerre* Phil Andros. It was one of these, called *Stud*, that Armistead was getting signed at a bookshop event. They exchanged pleasantries then Stewart signed the copy: 'To Armistead Maupin, one of the few successful tillers of the field. And in bed, WOW!' Understandably Armistead was not sure how to thank him for this but did his best. 'Well I'm not being presumptuous,' Stewart explained, reading his discomfort. 'I think this'll be useful to you in years to come. You'll be able to tell people that you slept with the man who slept with the man who slept with Oscar Wilde.' When Lord Alfred Douglas was well past middle age, young Sam Stewart had looked him up and seduced him simply so he could say he had and feel that sense of contact by proxy with a gay icon.

The novelist Tom Wakefield was always fond of saying that gay men had to help themselves because nobody else was going to do it. Armistead may not have slept with Oscar Wilde's grandtotty but the extended family he has built for himself reads like a gay Who's Who. The father of the group was Christopher Isherwood – surely a more reliable gay mentor than Oscar Wilde could ever have been. Forster and Maugham had helped him along, having doubtless been given similar hands-up in their youth, and he thought nothing of doing the same for Armistead. (Who, in turn, did it for me and a host of other writers trying to wear the gay label with pride yet not be sunk by it.)

He met Christopher and his lover, artist Don Bachardy, in 1978, not at a literary *soirée* but at an Oscar Night party thrown by a producer of *Saturday Night Fever*. 'I recognized Chris across the room because I saw a PBS documentary where he sat staring with those piercing blue eyes into the camera, completely intoxicatingly. And Don was very cute and boyish and Chris was in his cups but very charming.' Armistead dared to introduce himself then, when Isherwood said that he had enjoyed what he had read of *Tales*, dared to hit him for a blurb. 'He said he'd be more than happy to do it and he said, "I'm listed in the Santa Monica directory." He used to tell audiences that he was listed in the phone book. Extraordinarily brave.' The blurb Isherwood produced compared Armistead to Dickens. This was a highpoint of Armistead's life until recently, when he read Isherwood's diaries on the subject of blurbing his friend Dodie Smith's *I Capture the Castle*. He privately said the book was 'women's magazine stuff' but publicly compared it to ... Dickens. Armistead would see the couple intermittently either at his apartment or at the Isherwood-Bachardy house on Adelaide Drive in Santa Monica, where Armistead sat for portraits by Bachardy on several occasions. There were also numerous dinner parties served by their middle European maid, Natalie, a long-suffering soul whose demeanour was not unlike Lynn Redgrave's in *Gods and Monsters*. 'She had a sort of standard chicken and potatoes dinner. She would walk around while eight homos sat at the table buzzing about God knows what, and serve up the food without a word.' Armistead is ashamed to admit that he only came to Isherwood's work after seeing *Cabaret* and tracing it back to the source novels. 'And certainly there was an element of that in *Tales*; a nosy but loveable landlady, the notion of celebrating a city and the adventures of straight women and gay men. Chris and his writing were the same thing: direct and unpretentious and elegant and committed to clarity. His work was reader-friendly and unashamed of it.'

Isherwood in turn introduced Armistead to another startlingly honest friend, David Hockney, in late 1979. 'We all sat on grass mats at the Imperial Gardens on Sunset and that was the first time I was struck by the sort of ease and informality of their extended family.' Hockney became a firm friend and added Armistead's portrait to the series of colourful mugshots he produced in the late Eighties. The overlapping circles of gay influence became dizzying:

'When I first took Terry to Adelaide Drive, Don was off in another room. We immediately took snaps of each other in those famous straw chairs [from the Hockney portrait of Bachardy and Isherwood] because we were so acutely aware that we were on gay holy ground.'

Quite apart from giving *Tales* valuable support at a time when reviewers were ignoring it, Isherwood was the grandfather Armistead never had. 'Yet at the same time he felt like a contemporary. He never talked about the past. He was always chatting about the latest movie. I remember being there one night and him standing there in his preppy outfit — he wore these corduroy jackets with patches on the elbows, or a crewneck sweater and jeans. And he would bounce on his heels in a very energetic way. He was standing there and bouncing when Eddie Murphy came up. "Oh Eddie Murphy. Marvellous man! Marvellous man! Lovely lovely man!" And Rae Dawn Chong was there that night, the actress, and she said, "But Chris he's a terrible homophobe!" And he said, without missing a beat, "Well fuck him, then! Just fuck him!"'

For the *Village Voice*, Armistead wrote the final interview with the Isherwood-Bachardys before Isherwood's death and the publication by Faber of Bachardy's startling deathbed portraits of his lover. One abiding lesson Armistead retains from his mentor is never to let age be an excuse for moral cowardice. 'Chris had already arrived at the place that the rest of us were heading towards. And I always think of him when people use this generational excuse for failure of character: 'Oh it's just his generation.' But I'm sorry. If you're alive, you should still be growing. You should be figuring that out on your own.' The other lesson is, 'Do what you best know how to do.'

Celebrity has inevitably brought with it a certain caution about who is admitted to the family and how. It has also meant that the family is farther flung. If Isherwood was Armistead's father or grandfather, then his son, in gay political terms, is his close friend Ian McKellen, who, in fact, refers to Armistead and Terry as his godparents in his one-man show, *A Knight Out*. McKellen came through San Francisco in the early Eighties after the run of *Amadeus* on Broadway. A friend of Armistead's, Adam Block, who had befriended McKellen's then lover Sean Matthias during the shoot of *Priest of*

TERRY, ARMISTEAD, STEVE BEERY, STAGE MANAGER MITCH ERICKSON, AND IAN
MCKELLEN AT THE 50TH ANNIVERSARY CELEBRATION OF THE GOLDEN GATE
BRIDGE, 1988

Love in New Mexico persuaded Armistead to show McKellen the city.
Novelist and actor found themselves immediately in sympathy and arranged
for McKellen to repay the compliment when Armistead was next in London.
'I remember walking in on a sort of brunch party and sitting on a bench out
on the deck. And another actor, who was a longtime friend of Ian, had his
head in Ian's lap. And Ian was stroking his hair idly in a very Edwardian
Cambridge sort of way. It was a complete tableau. He was surrounded by
beautiful actresses who were completely comfortable around homos. It just
looked like the most wonderful circle of friends.' At this stage, McKellen was
only out to his friends, although his sexuality was an open secret among most
gay theatregoers. (Even teenage ones; a group of us came over all trembly
during pre A-level exposure to his *Macbeth* ...) However he was aware that he
was keeping silent on the subject during interviews. When he returned to San
Francisco in 1987 with *Acting Shakespeare*, he sat up with Armistead, Terry

and Steve over late-night champagne. 'And at one point we started off about the closet here, as we had a tendency to do – *still* have a tendency to do – and he looked at us very directly and said, "Do you think I should come out?" So we told him why we thought he should for the rest of the evening. And I remember thinking, 'What a charming rogue you are, Ian. You know that's what we want to hear so you're asking our opinion on the subject.' And I guess because I was so used to being bullshitted about that, that I didn't realize the real thing when it came along.' This was the era when Armistead found himself routinely described as 'novelist and gay activist' in the media, bewilderingly for someone who was never a manner-of-barricades. He had no idea McKellen would truly be thinking of him as a political mentor so it came as a surprise when McKellen rang up from England, all excited, because he had just come out on Radio Four when Peregrine Worsthorne was being more than usually homophobic. 'And I remember going on tour to Britain afterwards with Terry and seeing Ian looking very celebratory on the cover of *Gay Times* and inside he recounted the whole evening in San Francisco and what it had meant to him. We read it with tears rolling down our faces. And we felt as if we had a new-born baby on our hands!'

ON THE SET OF THE BLUE MOON LODGE ('THE WHOREHOUSE OF MY HEART')
FOR THE FILMING OF 'MORE TALES OF THE CITY', 1997

Tales on tv

The process by which first *Tales of the City* then *More Tales of the City* made it onto television is a gruelling and frustrating one familiar to anyone who has ever tried to attach funding to anything with no policemen, vets or nurses in it. Hollywood, as Armistead never tires of quoting, is the town where you can die of encouragement. And American television is merely Hollywood with uptight advertisers holding the other end of every cheque ...

Tales was first optioned in 1979 by an independent producer who had an understanding with Warner Brothers. When Warner Brothers placed a full page trade ad announcing the acquisition, Armistead was so gratified he had a tee shirt made which read *Soon To Be A Major Motion Picture*. His optimism was deflated when the producer introduced him to the proposed writer who spent an entire evening gushing about how faithful he would be to this wonderful novel before suggesting they make the gay gynaecologist a serial killer.

This was only the first of several disappointments. HBO owned the rights for most of the Eighties but the executive who had brought it in left and few people in the business will pick up goods perceived to be second-hand. Repeatedly *Tales* would be supported by women executives who had no power to get it past the inevitable man upstairs. Repeatedly there were requests that the characters, particularly the gay characters, be desexualized.

At last, in 1990, by which time the novels had became an established cult in Britain, a bidding war ensued between the Really Useful Picture Group and Working Title, each perceiving the makings of a no-less cultish TV serial. Armistead sold to Sarah Radcliffe at Working Title because he and Terry perceived the company to be more workmanlike and less pretentious than its rival.

He had no desire to write the scripts himself. 'I didn't want to say which of my children's toes had to be cut off.' At first the task fell to Howard Schuman, a writer and broadcaster for whom Armistead felt affinity and instinctive affection. During a previous book tour, Schuman had interviewed him on *The Late Show*. 'I was very impressed by how menschy and directly queer he was. And I remembered having admiration for *Rock Follies*.' Sadly, Schuman's scripts were deemed by Channel Four to have strayed too far in tone and content from the original material. The second choice writer was Richard *thirtysomething* Kramer, who had already written a film-length adaptation when the novel was the property of HBO. Kramer, too, had his problems, not least because he tended to insert long, self-analytical monologues into a story in which much of the fun arises from the characters' impulsiveness and *lack* of self-analysis. There was another problem. 'The technique, apparently, on the set of *thirtysomething* was for people to fight constantly and to argue and to hurt each other and to kiss and make up. Which bled into the scripts. It was a constant cycle. The rest of us were largely Southern or British. So with the possible exception of Terry, our whole instinct was to smooth the way and to get along with each other as best as we could through the creative process. Having said that, I was delighted with the script that Richard turned out.'

Tales also landed a dream cast, so much so that Armistead had the weird sensation of his imaginative 'family' taking on flesh and blood and becoming a second, real life family of his own. The principal reasons for this were his instant affinity with Olympia Dukakis and Laura Linney. The casting of Anna Madrigal had long been a fantasy for her many fans. Some people wanted a man, some wanted Bea Arthur. 'But in my mind she needed to have a sort of raw-boned grace, to be earthy and ethereal at the same time. For a while I thought that Gena Rowlands would make a very good Anna Madrigal, because she *has* that strong jaw and sort of mannish deportment but *is* very feminine inside. Anne Bancroft is another person who'd have been a more obvious choice.' Olympia Dukakis was Terry's brainwave. Traditionally she had played ethnic roles – Jewish or Italian mothers – but Terry pushed the idea until the choice became blazingly obvious to Armistead as well.

Laura Linney was initially auditioned for the part of DeDe Halcyon-Day, having already made a mark playing hard-edged characters. The original candidates for Mary Ann failed to work out for one reason or another so the casting director sent Armistead a tape of Laura. 'And my instant response was, "Why on earth didn't you give it to her the moment she walked in the room?" The perfect embodiment of Mary Ann. She knows how to project the innocence, the early innocence, and can also convey the notion that there are wheels turning behind those eyes.' Not only did Linney have an instinctive understanding of Mary Ann's irony, she was also – like Armistead – raised to be a people-pleasing Southerner and the two of them became fast friends, proving to have people in common in their backgrounds. Including a legendary dyke paediatrician who once lopped off a cadaver's dick with a scalpel, but that's another story ...

The sense of purpose was palpable on the set. 'With few exceptions the cast and crew were acutely aware that something groundbreaking was happening. And the pride we felt in doing it has lasted for a long time. Thomas [Gibson] and Barbara [Garrick] and Parker [Posey] all marched with me and Terry and our producer Alan Poul in the Stonewall 25 parade in New York after the show had aired. I realized this had been much more than a gig to them. They knew they were changing the world a little.'

The series was filmed on location and, by one of those strokes of serendipity, in the small LA soundstage where *Whatever Happened to Baby Jane* was filmed.Under the watchful eye of director Alastair Reid, 28 Barbary Lane was recreated as a huge set that dovetailed, on screen, into the San Francisco locations that had inspired the fantasy address in the first place. Being funded by Channel Four, there were few of the strictures commonplace on American TV about drugs or sex, so mention and shots of both abounded. It received a major promotion on bus stops across Britain, and tapped directly into a resurgence of interest in all things Seventies, particularly among viewers too young to remember them the first time around. The show received recognition as the year's best drama series by the Royal Television Society and, back in the States, the prestigious Peabody Award. In 1998 it was named one of 'The Hundred Greatest TV Shows Of All Time' by Entertainment Weekly Magazine.

More Tales of the City did not, however, go into immediate production. Far from it. Although the first series had been fully funded by Channel Four, PBS, America's non-commercial channel, purchased broadcasting rights in the States. Viewing figures were excellent and, for all the dope and raunchy plot lines, many Americans wrote in to say how refreshing it had been to see a well-made, well-acted series with no violence in it. Understandably, Channel Four were eager to collaborate with PBS on the funding of a second series and at first PBS were keen. Such was the fuss raised by Donald Wildmon and his reactionary American Family Association, however, particularly in the Southern states, that PBS caved in to pressure and withdrew their support. Channel Four, which for all its minority interests brief still has advertising to sell, did not feel the British viewing figures justified it funding a second series alone. Thus it took four years – and the persistence of producer Alan Poul – for *More Tales* to reach our screens in 1998, in a version funded largely by Showtime, the American cable channel, and shot in Montreal to comply with Canadian subsidy requirements. The script writer this time was English playwright Nicholas Wright who, like Kramer, would receive an Emmy nomination for his work. It was nothing short of a miracle that the any of the original cast were still available. The show had the same Mary Ann and Anna Madrigal, while Barbara Garrick, Thomas Gibson and William Campbell were still present as DeDe, Beauchamp and Jon. But in the best soap opera tradition, aliens appeared to have made off with and replaced Michael, Mona and Brian. Chloe Webb refused to play Mona again unless she was paid more money than everyone else and Paul Gross was unable to return as Brian on account of his new-found stardom as many a gay man's favourite Mountie in *Due South*. Marcus D'Amico, in a meeting with *More Tales* director Pierre Gang, said he was 'ambivalent' about returning to the role of Mouse, so was not invited back.

More Tales retained the set – which, farcically, had been dismantled and transported by train to Canada – the music, the not always intentionally brooding studio lighting and the tongue-in-cheek Hitchcockian spookiness of *Tales*. It also featured another cameo appearance by Armistead. He had cropped up in *Tales* as himself – peering grouchily up from his typewriter in a Barbary Lane window. This time he briefly took centre stage as a priest at

Grace Cathedral who is celebrating Communion when a severed human limb tumbles onto his altar at the moment of consecration. Terry, meanwhile, celebrated his dark side as one of the cathedrals' sinister cannibals ... Where the second series differed markedly from the first was in the cheekiness with which the scenes were peppered with sex, drugs and swearing. Liberated from all restraint, thanks to the series having a cable broadcast deal and a subsequent commercial video release, the makers seemed to be thumbing their collective noses at both PBS and the American Family Association. The *Chronicle* reported with glee that there were more bare male buns on display than in a branch of Burger King. The show was nominated for five Emmys – three more than the first series – but once again won none of them.

To Armistead's great distress, the Canadian production company of *More Tales* demolished 28 Barbary Lane after the shoot, insisting it would be more costly to store the set than to rebuild it for the next miniseries. But that moment may not come. At the time of writing, plans for the adaptation for *Further Tales* are mired in the same muddy processes that delayed the first two series.

DAVID HOCKNEY, TERRY, ARMISTEAD AND TV HOST JOAN QUINN AT A COSTUME
BALL IN SAN FRANCISCO, EARLY NINETIES

The celluloid closet

Armistead jokes that films and the closet are the two most important things in his life. In the last ten years, with his increasing involvement in the film and broadcasting industries, with actors and producers, the two preoccupations have become almost inseparable.

After the disappointment of the Emmys awards ceremony, the *Tales* team gathers at a restaurant table to lick its wounds. As well as Olympia Dukakis, who is predictably tired and eating nothing, having lost out to Ellen Barkin in a network TV movie, our table is joined by her stunning daughter plus date. The date is a cute young actor who begins by telling us at great length about the gay projects he's been working in and how much that has meant to him personally. He then begins to say how he's considering whether or not to reveal his homosexuality when the time comes to publicize the film. Armistead freezes over. Thank God Terry is talking to Gary and has not heard. The actor begins to kiss the girl's neck and she sighs prettily and confesses that he has asked her to marry him repeatedly. It's a chilling moment and typifies so much of what we discuss in our West Hollywood hotel the next morning.

> *'I've made rules about my life. I think I would have had success a lot earlier if I hadn't been so insistent about certain character requirements when it came to the closet. And in my paranoid moments, like this morning, I can tell myself I've pissed off too many people in this town to win that fucking Emmy because I've always been so demanding about honesty.'*

Armistead's preoccupations with the Hollywood closet have been brought to a head by two major working conflicts in recent years. One involving an actor from *Tales*, the other, Lily Tomlin.

The actor from *Tales* will remain anonymous in this account, because Armistead is wary of libel laws, which tend to be touchy about the mere discussion of homosexuality, especially in Britain. 'This has always been a major complaint of mine, that the law itself stigmatizes us, makes us officially different from the rest of humanity. I've tried to challenge that, being as matter-of-fact as I can as often as I can. On the other hand, I have no desire to subsidize this person's life for the rest of mine.'

'I'm sometimes asked why there are no major actors in Tales *who are openly gay, and I'm tempted to reply that we once thought we had such a person but were sorely disappointed. I've never specified that any of our actors be gay or openly gay, because I don't think that's fair to actors and I don't think that's fair to the show, because you want the best man or woman for the role. But it would have been a great political statement as well as a good hook for publicity and a wonderful opportunity for some young actor to come blazing onto the scene. So when the producers called me to say, "We've found this marvellous guy who projects a great deal of sweetness and sensitivity." I asked if he was openly gay and they said, "Well he certainly* appears *to be." The appearance was backed up by seeming fact when the actor not only joked with Armistead about all the cute guys on the set but asked for time off filming in order to march with thousands of gay and lesbian demonstrators in the March on Washington. 'Looking back, I guess he was just giving me what I wanted. It must have been one of the few times ever that an actor tried to look openly gay in order to please his producer.'*

The showdown came when a reporter from the *San Francisco Examiner*, having been briefed by Terry beforehand, showed up to interview the actor and launched in with typically San Franciscan directness with, 'So, I understand that you're out of the closet.' To the dismay of both Terry and Armistead, who were sitting within earshot, the actor immediately said that he wasn't gay, and, in fact, had a girlfriend. 'It was completely chilling. It was like having the rug pulled out from under *US*.' When the actor came around afterwards for the traditional last-night-of-shooting hugs he faced an inquisition when Terry said, 'I can't hug you after what you just did. You're a liar.' The actor said he had no idea what could have given them the idea that he was gay. 'So I said, 'Well, for one thing, you've slept with a lot of men.' And he said, 'Well that's *your* definition of it. I'm not gay. I have a girlfriend. That's just your agenda. I don't see myself that way.' He was very clearly protecting some career he saw blooming on the horizon that we had given him the entrée to. The terrible irony was I had fought this system of lies and deceit for years and now *I* had created a vehicle for one more person to do this. It was a terrible night. The guy was crying before it over. And we left him there. Just walked off. It was awful. I realized how little had changed in the business since Rock's day.'

Then there was the Lily saga. After his friend and fellow activist Vito Russo's death from AIDS, Armistead was proud to be involved in the screen adaptation of his masterly survey of gay moments in film, *The Celluloid Closet.* Long discussed while Vito was still alive, it would be a grand posthumous tribute. Vito had originally asked Armistead to ask Ian McKellen if he would read the narration for it, which McKellen said he'd be delighted to do. When producers Rob Epstein and Jeffrey Friedman approached Armistead to *write* the narration, they said that the consensus was that a British voice would not be appropriate, that a Hollywood voice, the voice of a star, would help steer the documentary into the mainstream. They were working with Lily Tomlin behind the scenes and she was already proving invaluable in persuading other stars to appear. When they mentioned the possibility of asking her to narrate, Armistead expressed misgivings that she had never stated, for the record, whether she was gay or not. 'I would have been perfectly happy for a civilized heterosexual to do it and we talked about Anjelica Huston and Alec Baldwin. The sexuality of the narrator didn't matter, really, as long as something called *The Celluloid Closet* didn't involve closeted behaviour. The whole point of the film was how unnecessarily squeamish Hollywood had been on the subject.'

Armistead said the decision should be theirs but warned them that he was extremely vocal on the subject of Lily's carefully maintained now she is/now she isn't stance, 'even in public gatherings where Vito was being interviewed and long discussions were held about when she was coming out.' So, Tomlin was hired and, to Armistead's joy, Epstein and Friedman informed him shortly before a studio session that she had decided to use the film as a vehicle for her coming out. 'She would do it as a sort of tribute to Vito. This moved me tremendously at the time. I felt that the moment had finally come and that this was a lovely way to make a nod to an old friend and a graceful way for her to do it. And a huge publicity coup for the show itself.'

Tomlin read narration that acknowledged her lesbianism. Footage was shot, but never used, in which she talked about how early women's prison films had thrilled her as a tomboyish teenager, affecting her mannerisms and dress. 'And so I created narration in which she said, "And some of those films had a very big influence on *one* little lesbian growing up in so-and-so ..." and then we would cut to her. And she read that into the mike, seemingly with great pleasure.'

The understanding was that Tomlin would write a coming out piece for *The Advocate* to tie in with the film's launch. At the New York Film Festival, however, where the documentary was screened, Armistead was told by the editor of *Out* magazine that Tomlin was giving no other interviews and that *The Advocate*'s piece was being very tightly controlled; to all appearances, the star had no intention of discussing her sexuality. 'I approached Rob and Jeffrey about this and it appeared to be true. I never understood whether or not I had been misled by Rob and Jeffrey or whether she had misled them or whether she had meant to do it at the time and later gotten cold feet or felt pressure from the people around her. But, whatever the reason, I felt completely *had*.'

Armistead fumed for several weeks and complained to everyone he knew. Word reached Michael Musto, the out gay gossip columnist on New York's *Village Voice* who rang Armistead and asked if he'd like to talk about it. 'I explained my disappointment and my anger as lucidly as I possibly could to him and he ran it pretty much as I'd said it. In depth ... It accepted the common knowledge of Lily's homosexuality. I mean, for Heaven's sakes, her name was written on the wall of the juice bar in the Castro as one of the great lesbian heroes. She's cultivated that for *years* within the gay community but completely side-steps it when it comes to talking to the mainstream press. Which only suggests, in a very old-fashioned way, that it's something to be ashamed of.'

Musto's piece ran but, surprise surprise, was only picked up and commented on by the gay press.

ARMISTEAD AND AUTHOR ALICE WALKER, CO-CHAIRS OF THE ANNUAL
FUNDRAISER FOR THE SAN FRANCISCO LIBRARY, 1998. 'WE LOOK SO MUCH LIKE
A COUPLE HERE THAT ALICE SAID I SHOULD SEND THIS HOME WITH A NOTE:
DEAR DADDY, THERE'S GOOD NEWS AND THERE'S BAD NEWS...'

Full circle

As this book goes to bed, Armistead finds he still draws strength and encouragement from his chosen family. Terry and Gary have just bought a home across the valley, fully visible from Armistead's office; as Terry wryly observes, 'Semaphore is entirely possible.' Armistead and Terry continue to dote on their godsons, Nicolas and Jasper Sheff, the children of writer, David Sheff and artist Karen Barbour, illustrator of the American editions of *Tales*. Others in the Armistead's circle include actor/writer James Lecesne, casting director Davia Nelson, and Pam Ling and Judd Winick, doctor and cartoonist respectively who met and fell in love while being filmed for MTV's fly-on-the-wall show, *The Real World*.

One of the great things about getting to be famous as well as getting to be the age you remember your father being, is that you stop being scared. Scared of your family. Scared of your hometown. It's comparatively easy to come out and live a gay old life when you live on the other side of a large continent. It's quite another to take the new gay you back to where – like me – you're likely to run into men you instinctively call Sir and women who remember you back when you wore shorts and a snake-belt and didn't yet realize why you preferred *Lost in Space* to *The Waltons*.

Even allowing for his battles with the American Family Association, Armistead has bearded the South and begun to reach an accommodation with his family heritage that *The Night Listener* will surely complete, however painful he finds the process. Arguably this process began back in the late eighties, when he and Terry were touring, very much as a high profile gay couple, to promote *Sure of You*. Armistead mentioned to Armistead Sr that they were coming through Raleigh and would like to call in. Sadly Armistead Sr and his second wife, Cheryl, were going to be away in China but

Armistead Sr said they'd be welcome to stay at the house anyway. Soon after, however, the offer was mysteriously withdrawn. To make matters worse, Tony was alerted to invite them instead. 'So my brother called me and said, "We'd love to see y'all. We've got two bedrooms you can have." And when I called him on that and said, "We're a couple, just like you and Jean," my brother said, "I know. I understand. I'd be insulted too. But we have two bedrooms you can have." I think they were afraid that their young daughter would be ruined by the sight of two men who loved each other and slept in the same room. We ended up staying at a hotel just to reclaim our dignity. So you know, this has been a long road for me. It's been very, very slow in terms of their complete acceptance, and it still bothers me that my father turns a deaf ear when people like Jesse Helms call people like me sinful and perverted. I don't think I'd let anybody say that about *my* son. And I certainly wouldn't vote for them.'

Nevertheless bridges have been built, not least through television, less the two miniseries than the awesome moment when Armistead was mentioned in a question on *Jeopardy*. The question master asked where Armistead Maupin's *Tales of the City* was set and some woman answered London but Armistead Sr was delighted. Being the subject of a *Jeopardy* question, after all, put Maupin up there with Jefferson and Babe Ruth.

Armistead, in turn, has grown much closer in recent years to his stepmother, Cheryl. 'She's my age, actually, so we have things we can talk about. She loves my father a lot, just as I do, but she doesn't take any shit from him and seems to have accepted that he isn't likely to change his way of doing things at 84.'

There's a delightful story of how recently Armistead Sr heard the news that Armistead had been invited to address a gay fundraiser in Haywood Hall in Raleigh - former ancestral home to a branch of his family. The old man tried touchingly hard to be PC and made noises to the effect of, 'Well that's just great, son,' until Armistead told him he had turned the invitation down whereupon Armistead Sr barked, 'Thank *God* for that!'

Armistead's sister Jane, now a full-fledged citizen of New Zealand, remains his best friend and his link to his biological family. 'We run up huge phone bills gossiping about Raleigh and Wainui and everywhere in between. She's a very kind person, like my mother, but as strong as my father – not a bad combination. And Tony has made a genuine effort to reach out in recent years. We're as wildly different as brothers can be, but we know that we love each other. He recently rescued a man from drowning during a flood, and was thanked by Bill Clinton himself. Tony was mortified to be on stage with a Democrat, but I was so proud of him.'

Interestingly, a number of family reconciliations seem to have occurred at Kahikatea. 'The local Maori regarded that part of the valley as enchanted – the fairies were said to live there – which wasn't lost on us, believe me, when Terry and I moved in. But there may some truth to it. It's been a very healing place for the family. Either that or it's just a lot easier to see each other as people without all those Raleigh ghosts around.'

Armistead and Terry had already faced down the disapproval of the Raleigh ghosts in 1988, when they agreed to lead Raleigh's first gay pride parade. 'We led the parade down the main drag in Raleigh, past the Confederate monument that had been erected by my great grandmother. And I made a speech on the steps of the Capital Building, the North Carolina State Capital Building, in which I condemned Jesse Helms, my former employer. And there was a wedding going on across the way at Christ Church at the same time. And the bells were ringing so loudly that we were convinced that they were trying to drown out the gay pride rally.'

Fat chance of that ...

TERRY, SEX COLUMNIST ISADORA ALLMAN, ARMISTEAD, AND THE AUTHOR AT A
WEDDING IN STERN GROVE, SAN FRANCISCO, 1988

And finally

As my overladen taxi grinds back to the airport, it strikes me there could be no finer way of letting Armistead have the final word than what follows. This 'blueprint for a more fulfilling life' appeared as part of the article Armistead wrote for *The Advocate* in 1985, which not only brought him and Terry together but proved one of the magazine's most quoted pieces ever. I make no apologies for quoting at such length; thirteen years on, if the likes of *Boyz* and *Attitude* are any gauge, there are still all too many who could do with having such wisdom glued on the bathroom wall in place of a mirror...

From: Armistead Maupin's Design For Living

1. Stop begging for acceptance. Homosexuality is still anathema to most people in this country – even to many homosexuals. If you camp out on the doorstep of society waiting for 'the climate' to change, you'll be there until Joan Rivers registers Democrat. Your job is to accept yourself – joyfully and with no apologies – and get on with the adventure of your life.

2. Don't run away from straight people. They need variety in their lives just as much as you do, and you'll forfeit the heady experience of feeling exotic if you limit yourself to the company of your own kind.

Furthermore, you have plenty to teach your straight friends about tolerance and humor and the comfortable enjoyment of their own sexuality. (Judging from 'Donahue,' many of them have only now begun to learn about foreplay; we, on the other hand, have entire resorts built around the practice.)

Besides, it's time you stopped thinking of heterosexuals as the enemy. It's both convenient and comforting to bemoan the cardboard villainy of Jerry

Falwell and friends, but the real culprits in this melodrama are just as queer as you are. They sleep with you by night and conspire to keep you invisible by day. They are studio chiefs and bank presidents and talk-show hosts, and they don't give a damn about your oppression because they've got their piece of the pie, and they got it by living a lie.

3. Refuse to cooperate in the lie. It is not your responsibility to 'be discreet' for the sake of people who are still ashamed of their own natures. And don't tell me about 'job security.' Nobody's job will ever be safe until the general public is permitted to recognize the full scope of our homosexual population.

Does that include the teachers? You bet it does. Have you forgotten already how much it hurt to be fourteen and gay and scared to death of it? Doesn't it gall you just a little that your 'discreet' lesbian social-studies teacher went home every day to her lover and her cats and her Ann Bannon novels without once giving you even a clue that there was hope for your own future?

What earthly good is your discretion, when teenagers are still being murdered for the crime of effeminacy? I know, I know – you have a right to keep your private life private. Well, you do that, my friend – but don't expect the world not to notice what you're really saying about yourself. And about the rest of us.

Lighten up, Lucille. There's help on the way.

4. Stir up some shit now and then. Last spring I wrote a commentary for the *Los Angeles Times* on the subject of television's shoddy treatment of homosexuality. The piece originally contained a sentence to the effect that 'it's high time the public found out there are just as many homosexuals who resemble Richard Chamberlain as there are who resemble Richard Simmons.' The editor cut it. When I asked him why, he said: 'Because it's libelous, that's why.' To which I replied: 'In the first place, I'm not saying that Richard Chamberlain is gay; I'm simply saying there are plenty of gay men who resemble him. In the second place, even if I were saying that Richard Chamberlain is gay, it wouldn't be a libelous remark, because I'm gay myself and I don't say those things with malice. I don't accuse anyone of being gay; I state it as a matter of fact or opinion.' When the new city of West Hollywood assembled its council last month, the Associated Press identified the three openly gay members as 'admitted homosexuals.' Admitted, get it? Fifteen years after the Stonewall Rebellion, the wire service wants to make it perfectly clear that homosexuality is still a dirty little secret that requires full confession before it can be mentioned at all.

If you don't raise some hell, that isn't going to change.

5. Don't sell your soul to the gay commercial culture. Well, go ahead, if you insist, but you'd better be prepared to accept the butt plug as the cornerstone of Western civilization. I am dumbfounded by the number of bright and beautiful men out there who submerge themselves completely in the quagmire of gay ghetto life, then wonder why their lives seem loveless and predictable. What the hell did they expect?

It you have no more imagination than to swap one schlock-heavy 'lifestyle' for another, you haven't learned a goddamn thing from the gay experience. I'm not talking about sex here; I'm talking about old-fashioned bad taste.

No, Virginia, we don't all have good taste. We are just as susceptible to the pitfalls of tackiness as everyone else in the world. Your pissing and moaning about the shallowness of other faggots falls on unsympathetic ears when you're wearing a T-shirt that says THIS FACE SEATS FIVE.

Not long ago I sat transfixed before my TV screen while an earnest young man told a gay cable announcer about his dream of becoming Mr. Leather Something-or-other. He was seeking the title, he said, 'in order to serve the community and help humanity.' He wore tit rings and a codpiece and a rather fetching little cross-your-heart harness, but he sounded for all the world like a Junior Miss contestant from Modesto.

If our fledgling culture fails us, it will be because we forgot how to question it, forgot how to laugh at it in the very same way we laugh at Tupperware and Velveeta and the Veterans of Foreign Wars.

6. **Stop insulting the people who love you by assuming they don't know you're gay.** When I began my book tour, a publicist in New York implored me to leave his name out of it, because 'my family doesn't know about my...uh, lifestyle .'

Maybe not, but they must be the dumbest bunch this side of Westchester County; I could tell he was gay over the telephone. When my own father learned of my homosexuality (he read about it in *Newsweek*), he told me he'd suspected as much since I'd been a teenager. I could've made life a lot easier for both of us if I'd had the guts to say what was on my mind.

7. **Learn to feel mortal.** If AIDS hasn't reminded you that your days are numbered – and always have been – then stop for a moment and remind yourself. Your days are numbered, Babycakes. Are you living them for yourself and the people you love, or are you living them for the people you fear?

I can't help thinking of a neighbor of mine, a dutiful government employee who kept up appearances for years and years, kept them up until the day he died, in fact – of a heart attack, in the back row of an all-male fuck-film house. Appearances don't count for squat when they stick you in the ground (all right, or scatter you to the winds), so why should you waste a single moment of your life seeming to be something you don't want to be?

Lord, that's so simple. If you hate your job, quit it. If your friends are tedious, go out and find new ones. You are queer, you lucky fool, and that makes you one of life's buccaneers, free from the clutter of two thousand years of Judeo-Christian sermonizing. Stop feeling sorry for yourself and start hoisting your sails. You haven't a moment to lose.

For more information on Armistead Maupin visit 28 Barbary Lane Online: **www.talesofthecity.com**